The Equation

Also by Omar Tyree

Pecking Order
The Last Street Novel
What They Want
Boss Lady
Diary of a Groupie
Leslie
Just Say No!
For the Love of Money
Sweet St. Louis
Single Mom
A Do Right Man
Flyy Girl

The Urban Griot Series

Cold Blooded
One Crazy Night
Capital City
College Boy

Anthologies

Dark Thirst
The Game
Proverbs of the People
Tough Love: The Life and Death of Tupac Shakur
Testimony

Children's Book

12 Brown Boys

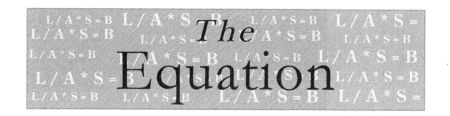

The
Equation

Applying the
4 Indisputable
Components of
Business Success

Omar Tyree

WILEY

John Wiley & Sons, Inc.

Dedicated to my mother

Renee McLaurin Alston
for teaching me the importance
of saving a dollar

And to my wife

Karintha L. Tyree
for showing me what loyalty
is all about

I woke up one morning
and asked myself the question
"What if?"
And once I thought about it
in detail
I decided to make "if"
a reality.
And then "if"
became this.

The Power of Creativity
By Omar Tyree

CONTENTS

THE GREEN SECTION
Support Is Pivotal

THE PURPLE SECTION
Business Is Royalty

THE WORKSHEET
The Equation in Use

The Power and Promise of Innovation

We want to continue to be innovative and aggressive about seeking customer input and using it to develop future Dell products. . . . Collaborative R&D between IT buyers, vendors, and partners is central to future innovation.
—Michael Dell writing in *Information Week,*
January 27, 2003

Whatever your placement in business today—as CEO, manager, intern, recent MBA grad, or entry-level employee—there is one word that should define, color, inhabit, and inform every single minute of your workday in the weeks, months, years, and decades to come. That word is *innovation.*

Innovation has been the central focus in my role as Vice President of Global Consumer Innovation for Dell, Inc. But *innovation* is not a new topic at Dell. It was in 1984 that an 18-year-old college student named Michael Dell had a bold idea for what would eventually become a company that has been a long-running member of the Fortune 50, with an ever-changing portfolio of innovative products and services sold around the globe. On some level, all *innovation* is entrepreneurship. Today, global leaders are looking for new ways to unlock the magic of the start-up on a daily basis inside of large corporations. The trick is how to do it.

Dell, Inc. has "an unwavering commitment to delivering new and better solutions that directly address customer needs" and uses three company-wide protocols to directly affect day-to-day operations: *listen, solve,* and *impact.*

To make *innovation* a daily event, we *listen* to "tens of thousands of customer interactions daily," *solve* "to deliver innovative and cost-effective solutions that meet today's real-life customer challenges," and *impact* consumers in such a way that "Dell spurs innovation and delivers value to customers."

Author Omar Tyree has discovered his own three protocols to infuse his love of writing, marketing, and entrepreneurship to drive innovation: *love, art,* and *support.* In turn, these three habits comprise *The Equation,* resulting in the sum of what he calls the "fourth indisputable component" of business. For Omar, a *New York Times* best-selling author, *innovation* isn't just something he does to be successful; it's what made him successful in the first place.

As Omar shows us in his masterful guide to loving what you do and doing what you love, *innovation* is not just an idea or a philosophy, but a daily practice put into use by the most successful, the most leading, and the most recognized businesspeople today.

In *The Equation,* Omar provides case studies of some of these master innovators, people like Momofuku Ando, creator of Cup Noodles, actor turned CEO Paul Newman, entrepreneur extraordinaire Richard Branson, and even Earvin "Magic" Johnson, who reinvented himself after a stellar basketball career to become one of the country's most respected and innovative businessmen.

How do they do it? How do these business leaders defy conventions, rewrite history, and make *innovation* a daily event for their companies, their employees, and themselves? To guide the work and reap the benefits of *innovation* in corporations today, I believe that success first hinges on leadership.

Leadership at the most senior level is a critical success factor—given the pressures on organizations to deliver financial results quarter after quarter—that shareholders and analysts expect of high-performing companies. Quite often, when organizations are faced with financial uncertainty, *innovation* is unfortunately the first to go. But I believe that burying an *innovation* group in the operations of a business is far from a recipe for continued success.

Innovation must be encouraged and supported, especially in large organizations.

Burying *innovation* is shortsighted thinking. *Innovation* groups need to be separate from daily operations. *Innovation* groups must be allowed the freedom to prosper or fail without being penalized.

I realize this thought process may seem counterintuitive to how corporations run today, but as *The Equation* shows over and over again, acquiring the freedom, the determination, and the courage to create innovative ideas has become a steady breeding ground for success.

In fact, in Dell's Consumer Division, we have aligned *innovation* reporting to the president of the business, who reports to the founder and chairman of Dell, Inc. And at the end of the day, our continued goal is to give global consumers new and innovative products that they can grow to love and depend upon.

With corporations now facing global warfare in the competition for profit margins—where cash is still king—*innovation* is still needed to produce first-to-market products that emerge only from a hands-on approach. *Innovation* gives businesses the sole promise of creating quality goods that consumers need.

Throw out the old rule books that claim *innovation* doesn't matter, and write one that starts with *innovation* first, where the day-to-day operations blossom as a result. That is the theory behind Omar Tyree's astounding and innovative look at global business in *The Equation.*

So as you read the following pages, pay heed to this one author's incredible story, and learn how *innovation*, courage, and vision will lead to greater business opportunities for us all.

—FENORRIS PEARSON
Vice President of Global Consumer Innovation for Dell, Inc.

The Same 4 Components

There are millions of successful businesses worldwide. There are millions of successful people who have established these businesses. And there are millions of different services and products of business to become successful in, with new innovations developed every year. But with every new or established enterprise worldwide, the same 4 components are utilized in a consistent and balanced formula to produce success. These same 4 components in their respectful order of execution are; *love, art, support,* and *business*. The consistent formula of their success, or what I call *The Equation* is

$$Love/Art * Support = Business$$

This equation was devised to establish these same 4 components of successful enterprise into a clear and focused science for us all to comprehend and utilize. So if you are interested in learning how to apply this worldwide technique to create, establish, expand, finance, or maintain a thriving and profitable business of your own, or to increase the success of your existing business, then you have just found the right vehicle. You will now discover, as I have, that these same 4 components of *The Equation*, as applied for success in business, are indisputable.

Many of you may not be familiar with the name Momofuku Ando or his international company, Nissin Foods, but if you have ever wandered into a convenience store late at night or early in the afternoon, looking for something hot and instant and walked out with a container or two of Cup Noodles, then you *are* familiar with Mr. Ando's midlife, million-dollar idea.

Momofuku, born Wu Baifu of Taiwanese heritage, was nearly 50 years old as he stood outside of a busy, black market food shop in Osaka, Japan, after World War II. He had become a Japanese citizen after the war, and he observed a long line of food-starved people awaiting a daily meal of hot noodle soup. With Japan still suffering from a shortage of food, Momofuku wondered if he could create instant noodle soup that would be immediately available to the masses. He claimed that "peace will come to the world when the people have enough to eat" ("Ando Was King of Instant Ramen," *The Japanese Times* Online, January 7, 2007).

After months of trial and error, in 1958 Ando perfected his historical method of cooking, drying, and packaging noodles to be enjoyed at anytime and anyplace. However, because normal noodles were available at Japanese grocery stores at a much lower price, Momofuku's new creation was deemed a luxury item for those who could afford it.

Ando stuck to his passion, established a new business, Chikin Ramen, and as his prices dropped, he was soon averaging thousands of daily orders in Japan. He then expanded his Nissin Foods start-up into the #1 brand of instant foods in a rapidly growing industry of imitators. In 1964, seeking a way to promote the instant noodle industry, Ando founded the Instant Food Industry Association.

By 1971, Momofuku Ando was recognized as the Ramen king. Nissin Foods then began to market and export what would become his greatest product, the patented Cup Noodle soup in a water-proof container. Americans fell in love with it, helping Nissin Foods to expand internationally. According to the company's web site, Nissin Foods now has 21,900 employees worldwide, operating 29 plants in 11 countries, while generating sales of more than $3.2 billion a year.

Applying *The Equation*, Mr. Ando envisioned an opportunity to create a business of *passion* based upon Japan's need for food and its citizens' *love* for hot noodle soup. He then set out to create an *art* of producing noodles that could be dried and packaged for quick, mass consumption. Once his new *art* form for creating instant noodle soup was mastered, along with the right price and marketing tools, Ando's community *support* in Japan began to grow enormously, spawning a new food industry. Multiplying his market throughout Japan and Asia, Nissin Foods soon secured a major import partnership with America, which increased its reach in *business* worldwide.

This first case study of many, explores the simple explanation and use of *The Equation*. But as most successful business people have learned, the execution of success is all in the details.

At the ripe age of 50, Momofuku Ando's creation of a worldwide instant noodle industry also shows that it is never too late to apply *The Equation* successfully. Great ideas often take time, dedication, and thoughtful planning to become fully developed. The details of *The Equation* as explained within this book are more than a decade in the making themselves.

I first began experiencing, understanding, and developing the concepts behind *The Equation* in the mid 1990s. At the time, I was an aspiring novelist in my early twenties with a passion for writing. As a member of the African-American community, I often wondered why there was so little contemporary literature with African-American characters and themes. So I took it upon myself to create them.

Finding no company willing to publish a recent college grad with ideas for novels, I formed a small company called MARS Productions, so that I could publish and distribute my debut novel, *Colored, On White Campus* in 1992. In consecutive years, I wrote and published my next two novels, *Flyy Girl* and *Capital City*.

Between 1992 and 1995, I sold more than 25,000 copies of my first three novels throughout Washington, DC, Baltimore, Philadelphia, New Jersey and New York, earning more than $160,000. In the spring of 1995, *Flyy Girl*, my second novel about a vivacious young woman who comes of age during the burgeoning hip-hop era of the 1980s, began to attract attention from major publishing houses in New York. And by the fall, I signed a two-book contract with a major publishing house in a six-figure deal, becoming one of the youngest African-American authors to secure a major publishing contract.

By my mid-twenties, having built my own publishing company with three novels and counting, I was a successful entrepreneur with a six-figure income. But despite what I had accomplished professionally, people perceived me more as a creative novelty than an actual business person. I was frequently asked the following questions: "Are you able to make a living from writing books? Do you have another day job? Do you write books full time? How long do you plan to do this?"

Their uninformed questions suggested that my writing career was little more than a passing hobby. In reality, I had been gainfully, self-employed as a writer even before signing with a major publisher. People failed to recognize that the publication and sales of my novels were sound business transactions. Publishing successful books was business, no matter how novelistic the idea seemed.

The opinions of many around me that my writing would land me one step out of the poor house didn't really bother me at first. I was never one to talk much about my personal income anyway. So I lived a simple life as a young man who rarely looked like he earned much money. I developed my relationships with professionals who worked in media, bookstores, distribution companies, and public libraries to expand my readership. And I continued to promote my books to the public with enthusiasm.

But when I began to be invited to high schools and colleges in the late 1990s, to lecture students on how to develop a writing career, I noticed that far too many students had an all-or-nothing idea of being imaginative. They had not been informed about the economic value of creativity in business.

While they understood that writing required skill and talent, many students, particularly those from underdeveloped communities, did not recognize writing or print journalism as valuable professions. These students viewed my career choice as a noble occupation more than an economically rewarding one.

Many professionals had the same idea. They believed that a writing career would not lead to a successful lifestyle. So I had to devise a way to debunk their misconceptions about creative careers.

Just as in any other profession, there is a hierarchy of income levels for writers. In every trade, there is a pecking order. But since many are not exposed to the infinite possibilities and aspirations of creative businesses, they have no way of knowing what the facts are. Infinite possibilities are not just the facts of writing books, they are an economic reality of *all* creative professions. Everyday innovators are consistently finding new ways to develop and focus their skills and creations, not only for their personal success, but for the benefit of the corporations and investors who employ or partner with them.

Passionate and innovative artists are not only writers and painters, they are also the designers of cars, homes, airplanes, clothing, retail stores, furniture, and computers that we all buy and use today. Other skilled professionals develop fragrances, grow fruit, create appliances, coordinate weddings, and plan special events. There are also specialized artists who create new inventions, medicines, tools, and marketable ideas.

Nevertheless, there seems to be a disconnect between the world of creative design and the business world of dollars and cents. The common stereotype portrays innovative artists as either broke and insane dreamers or very rich and lucky geniuses. There is no middle ground between the two. Perceiving these two extremes to be the only possibilities, the average individual is reluctant to explore the challenge of choosing a creative "career," and would rather choose a utilitarian "job" instead as being more practical.

It has now become my mission to show that there is a huge realm of success between these two extremes, where artistic people can live confident, comfortable, wealthy and productive lives as the creative forces within the business world.

Ironically, I began my own higher education at the University of Pittsburgh as a pharmacy major. Like millions of other students, I initially chose a career that I was familiar with. My mother worked in pharmaceuticals, and becoming a pharmacist was her passion. And although I became a Phi Eta Sigma Honor Society student while studying math and science prerequisites to enter the School of Pharmacy at Pittsburgh, I was not passionate about it.

I was a typical athletic, teenager from the inner-city of Philadelphia, with big dreams of becoming a professional football player. As an athletic walk-on student with no scholarship, I became a member of the Pitt Panther track team, secretly aspiring to join the football squad. Since I could not declare football as my major, I chose pharmacy, following in the footsteps of my mother.

Well, the football plans never materialized for me, and the pharmacy option faded into oblivion. But my proficiency in math and science would later allow me to come up with a formula to explain the connections between scientific process, business execution, and the emotional ideas of the creative arts.

After my second year at Pittsburgh, I transferred to Howard University in Washington, DC, changing my major from Pharmacy to English and finally Print Journalism. My instructors were amazed that I was able to transition from pharmacy's curriculum of math and sciences to writing's grammar and creativity.

I didn't think much of it at the time. All I knew was that I loved being able to add things up, figure things out, and explain my findings to others. So I found that the combined skills of math, science, literature, and public speaking were effective and valuable assets.

When I became a successful writer and entrepreneur, with a love of explaining my work to others, I began to educate students on how they too could become successful by pursuing their passions. I then studied the most important facts of success to communicate a solid and effective message, whether students wanted to be business professionals, football players, pharmacists, or astronauts. Surely they didn't all aspire to become writers. So I came up with the first component of *The Equation*.

All of the individuals I met, read about, or heard about, who were successful, happy, and productive in life, all seemed to *love* their professions. You could tell that they truly loved what they did. They spoke excitedly. Their eyes and body language were expressive. They showed tireless energy. And they could explain the various elements of their work with inspired details.

People who disliked or felt indifferent about their professions did not seem as satisfied with their lives, their income, or their personal status. They were constantly referring to other professions as the "dreams" that they "really" wanted to pursue, while claiming their everyday "jobs" as the "practical" career choices that I explained a few pages ago. These "jobs" were merely a way to survive and pay the bills, while they hoped for an unforeseeable lottery win to save them from their mundane existence. Predictably, their performances at work were generally weaker as well. They didn't have the same zest for life as the successful "career" people who loved their professions. But the "job" people had plenty of excuses to explain why.

In my lectures, I began to refer to them as the "coulda-woulda-shoulda people." I "coulda" done this, I "woulda" done that, and I "shoulda" done the other thing. Unfortunately, there are millions of people who continue to fit this category. We all have to do what we need to do to survive, right?

Well, if all you want to do in life is survive, then I guess you need to settle in comfortably with whatever it is you get in life and refrain from complaining about it. But if you actually want to enjoy your life and reach for some of your loftier goals or dreams, a better idea would be to learn how to achieve your aspirations, no matter how afraid you may be of your initial failures. Fortunately, successful people are curious and courageous. So keep reading.

After I concluded that successful people *love* what they do, I then realized that thousands of other people may *love* to do the same thing. How many young men around the world would *love* to have a career playing professional sports, in football, basketball, baseball, or soccer? Nearly every kid who plays recreational sports would love to turn pro one day, including my two eager sons. So the second component of *The Equation* had to address the reality of competition.

Competition is a hard fact of life. The more people who *love* to do the same thing, the steeper the competition gets for a career in that particular field.

However, I didn't feel that the term "competition" accurately described the second component of *The Equation*. The idea of competition only addressed a part of the concept. The bigger picture needed a more expansive word. So I continued to brainstorm for a more valid term.

A better word revealed itself through hearing repeated conversations about one of the greatest professional athletes in the world: Mr. Michael Jeffrey Jordan, the star of the six-time world champion Chicago Bulls. Sports commentators and newscasters spoke of Michael Jordan as the epitome of competition. And in the mid 1990s, they began to state that Michael Jordan turned the game of basketball into an "art form." He had become one of the all-time bests in his profession, like Picasso, Van Gogh, Beethoven, Bach, Ali, Tyson, Pelé, Beckham, Ruth, Aaron, Kubrick, Spielberg, Namath, Brown, Cruise, Smith, Sinatra, Davis, Streisand, Ross, Rockefeller, Gates, and a select group of others who had become not only competitive, but recognized as the very best at what they do. They had become worldwide "artists" revered for their greatness and ambition.

That was the word I was looking for. It was only three letters long and sat right in front of me the whole time: *art*. Can you become the best "artist" at what you do in life? Or if not *the* best, then *one of* the best. In other words, amidst all of the competition within every profession, how do we find ways to stand out and perform as valuable individuals?

Individuality is another form of strength. I've often heard it said, while growing up in crowded row house community of West Philadelphia, "God bless the child who's got his own."

It's one thing to compete with everyone, but it's much different to be the first one, the only one, or one of the few to compete within a select group. So how do you manage to separate yourself from the pack to become regarded as independent and special? That is the essence of *art*, to become individually skilled.

It takes great reserves of courage and self-discipline to achieve the goal of rarity. Many people are even terrified at the thought of the anxiety-filled heights where great *art* may take them. Once they reach the top of that steep climb of excellence, they realize that there is no easy way to back down. However, successful people find ways to fight through personal fears and public pressures to climb those mountains anyway. And at the end of the day, they would rather stand at the top, alongside the victorious few, then to stand in a crowd at the bottom afraid to climb.

With these first two components of *The Equation* in place, I began to apply sample numbers to see if my ideas made any sense.

When we say that we *love* something, typically we think of great amounts or high numbers. In grade school, the highest number was 100 percent, or an A grade. You could score more points with extra credit: 105 percent or 110 percent. Any grade above 90 percent was considered an A. Under the A grade was the B grade, from 80 to 89 percent. The C grade was from 75 to 79 percent. The D grade, or barely passing, was 70 to 74 percent. Any grade less than 70 percent was failing, or a grade of F.

In college, we were often graded on a curve, but the curve was still based on a scale of A, B, C, D and F, from the highest grade to the lowest grade. There was also a median, where the average grade fell in the middle of the curve. The median was generally regarded as a C. But who wants to be only average? Not successful people. Successful people plan to execute above average.

Assigning numbers to physical energy and emotions, I theorized that *love* should never be based on failure. The component of *love* should always be associated with the highest percentage, or 100 percent. To be successful, people must ask themselves, "How much do I *love* what I do?" A person who loves her profession only 50 percent of the time will likely not be a top performer.

By the same token, the concept of *art* is often likened to a rarity or a precious item that is represented by the lowest number. Most serious artists aspire to stand out and become special in their particular fields. They're not thinking about being one out of a thousand. They are more likely to set goals to become the #1 talent in their profession, or regarded within the Top 3, Top 5, or Top 10. Being grouped with a thousand others would make an artist feel less than special. So artists often compare themselves only to a select group of others who are considered the best, or regarded as unique in their skills.

Once the idea of assigning a high number to the variable of *love* and a low number to the variable for *art* made sense, I then used my background in mathematics to begin to formulate the rest of *The Equation*. Using *love* (L) as a *numerator* (the number above a fraction line to be divided into parts) and *art* (A) as the *denominator* (the number below a fraction line that represents the divisor), I concluded that a high number (100 percent) divided by a low number (1) would equal the highest *quotient* (the number produced by dividing a given number by another).

In other words, a person who loves what they do 100 percent and has toiled to become number one in their field, will produce a high *quotient number* (QN); as in 100/1 (L/A) which equals 100. As I ran *The Equation* through various examples, I realized that the theory worked perfectly. If a person only loves what they do at a 50 percent rate, and they land somewhere in the Top 35 in their field, 50/35 equals 1.43, a much smaller *quotient* than 100. But if a person loves what they do at an 85 percent rate, and they are regarded in the Top 5 of their field, 85/5 equals 17. Of course, 17 is a much lower *quotient number* (QN) than 100, but it is also 10 times higher than 1.43.

So far, so good, right? However, I realized that no matter how much you *love* what you do, or how much your high rank of *art* inspires or pleases others, *love* and *art* alone do not create success, wealth, or business. Devising your *quotient number* (QN) is only a start, but indeed a strong foundation to build on.

Now we arrive at the action part of *The Equation*. As much as I hate to say it, many artistic individuals have been stereotyped by the math, science, and business professionals as lazy slackers who don't appreciate real work and toil. And while math, science, and business majors are forced to register 18 to 22 credit hours a semester in colleges and universities, the liberal arts majors are often able to get by with only 12 to 15 credits with endless hours of free time before graduating with no immediate job in sight where they can apply their skills.

Nevertheless, math, science, and business majors need artistic products if their expertise is going to mean anything. What is the use in knowing how to add, subtract, multiply, and divide without having anything to add, subtract, multiply, or divide? In other words, what is the reason for the math? The reason for the math is to account for the business of human products, such as food, shelter, clothing, merchandise, and entertainment.

Well, there are farmers who are the artists of food, architects who are the artists of shelter, fashion designers who are the artists of clothing, engineers who are the artists of merchandise and technology, and singers, dancers, musicians, and actors, who are all artists of inspired performances and entertainment.

What is the use of science if it is not used for the betterment and understanding of the people, places, animals, phenomena, and things; organic (living) and inorganic (nonliving) of city, state, nation, continent, world, universe and galaxy? Although many of us may claim not to use or to think much about science, there is science in everything that we do. And when I say "we," I mean every person who has ever lived or died, because living (organic) and dying (inorganic) are still science.

There is also a science to how people react to *love* and *art*, which includes their reactions to different shapes, sizes, colors, scents, textures, tastes, sounds, moods, languages, cultures and so on. Even this book is science, the full explanation of an idea to be published, read, reviewed, debated, studied, learned, taught and utilized by the few or by the many.

This is where the world of *business* comes into play. No matter how indifferent those with the keys to wealth, in the forms of hard cash, bank loans, lines of credit, or investor capital, who wear business suits and ties, while carrying briefcases filled with budgets, sales goals, and business plans are to those who are not forced to wear a daily uniform or understand the basic principles of a balance sheet, there is no business without some form of creative product.

Stocks, bonds, investments, and the idea of money itself, are all based on placing numeric values on tangible goods. This means that if there are no Ford automobiles, Microsoft computers, Paramount Pictures, Verizon Wireless cell phones, Sony Walkmans, Dole pineapples, Armani suits, Dallas Cowboys, Atlanta Braves, Harris Teeter groceries, Warner Brothers Music, diamonds, silver, and government currency backed by gold, then there are no businesses, no stocks, no bonds, no money, no retirement funds, and no paychecks.

In fact, there are no jobs without the creation and sales of products and services. Even school systems need books, desks, chairs, blackboards, pencils and paper that are designed and created by artists. However, since few artists can afford to mass produce their creations, one has to surmise that the logical link between *love, art* and *business* is *support*.

Without question, monetary, community, and professional *support* is the most pivotal component of *The Equation*. Support is the bridge to all wealth and successful business. And unless an artist is fortunate enough to be born into a wealthy family, live within a supportive community, or is backed by a group of supportive professionals, he must find a way to attain that *support*.

Fortunately, I learned what hustle and focusing on the details was all about early in my career. Along with my academic schedule and athletic participation, I became a dormitory barber, who later worked a 40-hour-a-week job as a security guard to help pay for the final two years of my education. By 1991, when I graduated from Howard University with honors in Print Journalism, I went right after the prize of releasing my first novel through the *support* of African-American readers.

Fresh out of college at the tender age of 22, I took my educational investment seriously and immediately launched myself into business. I *loved* to write, and I was an *artist* who wanted to stand out with his gift. I also understood *business* and the value of earning a dollar. How could I not? I had paid for nearly half of my $50,000, four-year education. Since I had already written two books by the time I graduated, I wanted desperately to publish them. So I founded my own publishing company using personal savings, small loans, and cash gifts from my parents, relatives, friends, and from any small business associates who dared to *support* me.

Ten months and $3,500 later, at age 23, on October 6, 1992, I published my first book, *Colored, On White Campus*, with 1,000 copies to sell. I found myself $1,800 dollars in debt, but it was no sweat to me. I was happy to be in *business*. So I attended every book and *art* expo event to make back everyone's money through aggressive book sales. And I must admit, I was a rather brash young salesman, who rarely took no for an answer. I sold my first copies furiously. The more books I sold, the more it turned people on to me.

Five months later, in February of 1993, I had sold enough books to pay back my small niche of investors. I then asked them to roll the dice to *support* me again on my second book. Why not? I had a successful track record now.

In April of that same year, I published *Flyy Girl* and turned 24. I then quit my job as a reporter and writer for a small Washington, DC, newspaper, and went on to make history in the world of books and publishing.

My passion to create contemporary African-American novels eventually led to a multimillion-dollar niche industry of urban fiction and street lit, with its own dedicated sections in book store chains across the country today. Summing up the details of my lessons learned in school, in personal evaluations, and in the business decisions I made to become a success, the complete formula of *The Equation* became

$$Love/Art * Support = Business, or L/A * S = B.^{TM}$$

It was the same 4 components used by Momofuku Ando to create his empire of instant noodle soup in Japan after World War II.

I then began to test this new idea during the lectures I gave at high schools and colleges as early as 1997. I told the students, "First you have to select a field of work where you *love* what you do (L), then you work hard to become a highly skilled *artist* at it (A), while developing promotional and marketing tools to gather the *support* (S) that you will need to produce a successful *business* (B)."

I made examples of brave student volunteers and applied *The Equation* to their own dreams and aspirations so they could all see how the formula worked. The students and instructors got the idea and loved it. But as the saying goes, "Knowing is only half the battle." How many of us will actually apply *The Equation* successfully once we comprehend it and have read all of the details?

Since it took me more than a decade to finally land a deal to publish this book, I have now had plenty of time to fortify all of its concepts. And the more I enhanced *The Equation* over the years, the more I found that these same 4 components of successful business were indisputable. But since this is only the introduction, I will save the rest of the details for the main chapters.

THE EQUATION

$$L \, / \, A \, * \, S \, = \, B^{\text{TM}}$$

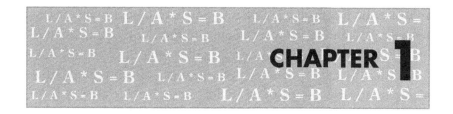

CHAPTER 1

A FURTHER EXPLANATION OF L/A * S = B

More than just a gimmick in a self-help business book, the proven formula of *The Equation* is a universal tool that illustrates how being passionate about your profession can significantly increase the quality of your skills, products, and services. Your devotion to excellence will then increase attention and public support, which ultimately translate into a successful business.

It doesn't get any simpler than that. My goal now is to map out the process for everyone. I believe that we are all artists in some way. Some people just have to find out what they're good at and put their all in to it. My *art* is to explain how it's done.

First, we must all understand that each and every one of us will play a necessary role in the development of a successful enterprise. Some people will *love* the product, inspire its creation, and provide the raw energy toward its production. Others will master the *art* of creating and improving the product to make it desirable. You will then need individuals to *support* the production, promotion, and sales of the product. Once these three components of *love,* *art,* and *support* are all at work in unison, the fourth component of *business* multiplication and progress is inevitable.

With the many start-up businesses of entrepreneurs—including myself—some of us are forced to execute all 4 of these components on our own. We then gain first-hand experience in evaluating the importance of them all. However, we all have our strengths and weaknesses. And we are at our strongest when able to assess what those strengths and weaknesses are, while making adjustments accordingly. *The Equation* will help us all to do so.

Since few of us are able to perform all 4 of these components on our own successfully, it is important to concentrate on your strengths, and then seek to partner with those who are able to balance out your weaknesses. Even if you are one of the fortunate few who is able to master all 4 components, the idea of progress in *business* is to eventually form larger teams of success called companies. These companies then become small or large depending on personal preference, ambition, available capital for expansion, and overall execution.

Utilizing *The Equation* will allow you to assess your individual efforts as an entrepreneur, the success of a growing company, as well as the contributions of its employees. But how can you realistically gauge how much people, as individuals, *love* their profession, how good they are at their particular craft, how much *support* they are able to gather, and ultimately, how much *business* they are able to generate?

Well, with *art* (A), companies use professional opinions, extensive research, public surveys, and rankings to determine artistic value. For team *support* (S), they make staff and management evaluations. For public *support* (S), they compute sales figures, overall attendance, raised funds, or tallied votes. And *business* (B) speaks for itself in the forms of increased products and services, as well as the obvious accumulation of revenue. But *love* (L), how do you ever account for love? And how many people will accurately grade themselves on a 100 percent scale, the way they did in grade school?

So I devised a comprehensive set of questions to ask prior to applying *The Equation* that will enable you to grade yourself more accurately and honestly. Although these estimates can never be exact—due to the natural imperfection of human judgment—they can indeed serve as clear representations of your individual and company value if used correctly.

This set of expanded questions is referred to as The Five Elements of each component—*love, art, support,* and *business.* The goal of defining the various elements that comprise each component is to ensure that the numerical value you assign to each variable is as accurate as possible. Using The Five Elements of each component, and the charts supplied in the final section, *"The Equation in Use,"* you will be able to make a more precise assessment of where you stand in your career within a given time period, career goal, or career aspiration. And as instructed, you may also create your own Equation Chart to apply to personal and or company needs.

For *love* (L), The Five Elements are *passion, commitment, dedication, loyalty,* and *consistency.* Based on the definition of each element of *love* (L), you will be asked to honestly assess the overall passion that you have in your career from 0 to 100 percent, and or assess the overall passion of your company.

For *art* (A), The Five Elements are *adoration, presentation, purpose, execution,* and *excellence.* Based on the definition of each element of *art* (A), you will be asked to assess your Competitive Rank within your professional field from 1 to 50, and or assess the Competitive Rank of your company within its industry.

For *support* (S), The Five Elements are *attraction, packaging, organization, imagery,* and *movement.* Based on the definition of each element of *support* (S), you will be asked to estimate the Supportive Range of your enterprise within a *communal, local, regional, national,* or *world* market, and or estimate the Supportive Range of your company.

Once you are able to input all of the necessary variables of *love* (L), *art* (A), and *support* (S), with use of the charts supplied in the final section, *"The Equation in Use,"* you will then be able to compute your Business Equivalent Number (BEN), and/or the

Business Equivalent Numbers of your company that apply to the chosen time periods, goals, and/or aspirations.

Your Business Equivalent Number is the calculated amount of Business Energy (BE) that is produced by an individual or a company within the worldwide market of people, products, and services.

Using the final calculations of your personal and or company BEN within *The Equation* Chart, you will be asked to input your personal *income* and or company *revenue* to calculate your *income value* and or *productivity value.*

Your personal and or company *income value* is based on the percentage of Business Energy (BE) that you or your company are able to secure in profits. Your personal and or company *productivity value* is based on the percentage of Business Energy that you are able to secure in profits from your company, and or the percentage of Business Energy (BE) that your company is able to secure in profits within its respective industry. These calculations will all be explained in detail in the final section, *"The Equation* in Use."

The completion of *The Equation* Chart will then allow you to evaluate, with clarity, The Five Elements of *business* (B), which include *income, productivity, progress, power,* and *responsibility.* And based on the definition of each element of *business* (B), we can then decide individually, what our new personal and or company goals and aspirations are, how we plan to execute our ongoing business, create new business, or how we plan to respond to the respective communities that surround and support us.

In addition, each component will be identified by a representative color.

The Equation itself is represented by the color black, as will be discussed in the following chapter. *Love* (L) is represented by the color red. *Art* (A) is represented by the color gold. *Support* (S) is represented by the color green. And *business* (B) is represented by the color purple.

$$L/A * S = B^{TM}$$

or *Red/Gold * Green = Purple*

Since printed colors may not always be available for each component, I have also devised the inclusion of a *symbolic image.*

Love (L) is represented by a *red paper cup.* *Art* (A) is represented by a *gold pyramid.* *Support* (S) is represented by a *green basket.* And *business* (B) is represented by a *purple wine glass.*

For those who accept the challenge of complete understanding, you will find that this universal formula of *The Equation* can be applied to each and every aspect of your business life. And for those of you who may be slightly intimidated, confused, or unconvinced by its use, I will now walk you through a detailed explanation, chapter by chapter.

CHAPTER 2

WHY THE COLOR BLACK?

The color black is a classic color. It is the color of permanence. In the ultraviolet spectrum of colors, black is classified as being without light, or the opposite of light. Where light shines on and illuminates most other colors, black is what is it and will be what it will be, with or without light. It is a solid in its most concentrated form. And there is no substitute color that is more permanent than black.

The color black is the beginning and the ending of all ideas. In the cavern of deep thought, black represents infinite possibilities. In light of illumination, it becomes the completed objective. So to mark any idea in the permanent color of black is to be taken seriously.

$$1 + 1 = 2 \qquad e = mc^2 \qquad L/A * S = B$$

For a scientist, the color black is the accepted law—the reality of life, death, and all of the unknown. For a mathematician, a teacher, or a writer, it is the mark of the question, the answer, and the documentation of the lesson. For a doctor, the often-used term, "black and blue," becomes the stimulus for evaluation, prescription, and a successful remedy for healing. For artists, architects, or engineers, the color black is the outlined sketch from which all of their ideas are created. And for a businessman, black is the bottom line, the goal of their capital, and the purpose of their interests. In other words, *What is the concrete (black) value of my investment?*

The color black is and will always be a constant. So if you plan to be successful in business, then write it down, take yourself seriously, and bring your ideas into existence.

The Equation is written in black ink. The challenge to understand it, appreciate it, respect it, and utilize it is now yours:

$$L/A * S = B^{TM}$$

LOVE WHAT YOU DO

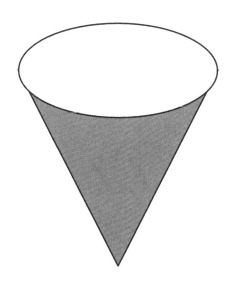

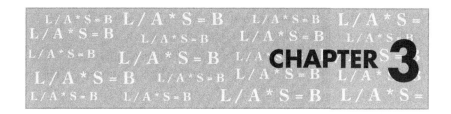

CHAPTER 3

THE DEFINITION OF LOVE

Love is the first indisputable component of *The Equation*, and is indicated by the color red. As an internally produced emotion, *love* is also inexpensive, as symbolized by the image of a simple *paper cup* that is to be filled to capacity. We are all capable of experiencing the inspirational forces of *love*, and it is gained through a multitude of sources. Therefore, *love* is the initiator of all success. And with the understanding of The Five Elements that make up this component, you will be able to determine your *numerator score*, or the initiating variable of business.

Webster's Third New International Dictionary defines *love* as attraction, desire, or affection felt for a person who arouses delight, admiration or elicits tenderness, sympathetic interest, or benevolence. The dictionary also states that *love* is a warm attachment, enthusiasm, or devotion as to a pursuit or a concrete or ideal object.

Since *The Equation* is concerned with business, we will refer more to the second definition of *love*. The questions then becomes this: How warmly are we attached to our objectified pursuits? How enthusiastic are we about our career goals? And how devoted are we to complete our specific journeys toward success? In other words, *"How much do we love what we say we love?"*

Love is the first component of *The Equation* because it is based in truth and can be measured in raw energy. The evidence of *love* is most obvious. Our actions and emotions are nearly impossible to deny. With the uninspired efforts often accepted within the workplace, one has to wonder how many of us are honestly involved in career pursuits that we *love*. That is a very serious question to think about.

We must first be honest with ourselves in what we actively pursue as the business of our lives. It is only natural for us to select careers that keep us emotionally fulfilled. However, many people have not chosen to pursue the obvious aspirations that would bring them the most attachment and enthusiasm.

There are millions of people who are not warm with *love* in their professions, many of whom lean toward career goals that are based more on proximity, expectation, and income.

After pursuing professional football, I had briefly chosen to pursue a career of pharmacy, not because of *love*, but because I was familiar with it. Others make career choices out of proximity as well.

Expectation can be another deterrent from selecting careers based on *love*. Members of certain societies are often expected to follow in the footsteps of their parents, friends, relatives or the working people around them whether they have *love* for the same professional goals or not.

Other people choose career goals based on income, another popular mistake. These individuals then claim to *love* making money. But is making money in the wrong field of work beneficial to them as a career goal? I would argue that in the long term, it is not.

As an award-winning author, a professional journalist, and a lecturer, I talk to many aspiring writers. They dream of becoming wealthy, with film deals and books on the *New York Times* best-sellers list. I tell them that their quest for riches, widespread recognition, and Hollywood fame will not make them successful writers. You must first *love* the craft of writing itself, as well as have something worthwhile, and unique to say. Everything else will fall into place as a product of your *love*.

Nevertheless, many continue to bypass this first essential component and end up chasing career goals that deplete the same energy, ingenuity, drive, and the stamina necessary to succeed.

As the popular saying goes, "*love* conquers all." One may argue that the popular cliché is not always true, but it is based on one's ability to strive towards goals despite turbulence and hardships. Those who *love* their mission *more* are likely to maintain their desire through the trials, setbacks, and letdowns along the way. However, those who *love* their missions *less* have a tendency to jump ship as soon as their ideas refuse to work as planned.

Individuals who have careers based on survival are in an even worse position. They find themselves locked out of opportunities even to choose the path they would like to follow. But at least they can be honest with themselves about their real interests. Survivalists are fully aware that they are not involved in what they would *love* to do for a living. However, their lack of *love* can also lock them into a fickle position of employment, where they are usually the first to be fired when the company starts to downsize.

In the twenty-first century, profitable industries are now engaged in more cost-effective ways of doing business. As a result, they are using advanced machinery, independent contractors, and outsourcing to other companies to produce more of their services and products. In that arena, a survivalist mentality—"I just do whatever I have to do to get by"—is the most suspect. Successful companies are no longer interested in survivalists, they're interested in specialists—people who know *exactly* what they're doing and who hold themselves accountable for their work. And more specialists *love* what they do than not.

So if you find that you *love* nothing in particular, then nothing in particular will *love* you. That's a hard, uninspired way to live and a sure recipe for failure in everything.

Do you *love* your career? How honest are you with yourself? Are you a survivalist, or do you honestly work for a higher goal?

Under public, societal, and common peer pressure, individuals often respond to tough questions about their goals by creating grandiose pictures of themselves to relate to others. It's a natural defense mechanism. But it's much easier for people to talk about what they *love* than to show it. However, the truth remains that *we are what we do* more than what we want to admit.

Love creates the substance of our individual character. Taking a look at an inspiring example, set by the late actor Paul Newman, will allow us all to glimpse what a successful business based out of *love* is capable of achieving.

In 1982, Newman and his friend, author A. E. Hotchner, founded a food company they conveniently branded as Newman's Own. Starting with a bottle of salad dressing that displayed the actor's image on the label, the company soon expanded to include spaghetti sauce, iced tea, lemonade, fruit cocktail juices, microwave popcorn, salsa, cookies and pet foods, all bearing the actor's recognizable image.

Newman and Hotchner created the company out of compassion, with the idea of building a vehicle that could help donate funds to charitable causes around the world. So instead of taking their company profits to the bank, the entrepreneurial franchise has donated its more than $200 million in earnings to charitable organizations, most notably to the Hole in the Wall Gang Camp for seriously ill children, established in Ashford, Connecticut, in 1988. The Association of Hole in the Wall Camps, an independently formed charity, has since raised funds to serve more than 13,000 children, and has paid their expenses to enjoy summer camp.

Having no idea how the company became so successful, Newman called it luck. Nevertheless, the spirit of their giving, and Paul Newman's identifiable face, which now appears on the packaging of mints, coffee, royal tea, dried fruit, chocolate bars, and cereal, has won over a loyal base of customers through grocery store chains across the country. His Newman's Own web site sells hats, T-shirts, sweatshirts, and copies of signed letters. The web site also lists a display of healthy food recipes, all to continue the popularity and growth of the brand in order to donate more of the company's gains to charity.

In regards to his contributions to benefit seriously ill children and other charitable causes, Newman simply stated, "Those who are most lucky should hold their hands out to those who aren't."

Now that's a business of *love*!

But imagine if we *all* could choose a career goal to love instead of a day job to hate? What if we *all* gave 100 percent effort toward the better good of humanity like Paul Newman? What kind of world would we live in if that happened? It would be an amazing sight to see, that's for sure. But realistically, if we can't count on the whole world to *love* what they do and to fill up their *paper cups* with effort, we can at least count on ourselves to *love* what *we* do and fill up our own cups. In other words, use the most accessible tool in business you have to offer—yourself.

CHAPTER 4

WHY THE COLOR RED?

Red is the color of *passion*. It is the color of blood, guts, radiance, and war. It conveys pure intensity. There is no halfway mark with red. Red is an all or nothing color. You can't walk into a room wearing the color red and not be noticed. Red is a signifier of decisive action; either you're in or you're out; either you love it or you hate it.

Red forces us to be honest about our intentions, and it intimidates the weak at heart. But for the courageous, it is invigorating; it enlivens us. Red wakes us up and gets us going, making us rise to the challenge.

Red means serious business. It is therefore necessary that we each find that passionate goal that makes us individually red. What turns you on? What gets you going? What makes you respond? If you have no red in your life, what are you waiting for! This Red Section of *The Equation* will explore those elements of *passion* that force us all to react, like the reactions created by the Italian race car founder, Enzo Ferrari.

Known as man of flamboyance and a fiery temper, Ferrari and his world-famous race teams and cars are as red as it gets. Even hearing the name Ferrari creates thoughts of speed and *passion*. One quick look at the internationally known and desired race cars can make even slow drivers imagine themselves racing down an open expressway in reckless abandon. However, the red *passion* of the Ferrari brand started with a driven young man of uncompromising vision.

Born in 1898 to a middle-class family in Modena, Enzo Ferrari had three ambitions: opera singer, sports journalist, and race-car driver. But after losing his father and brother in World War I, with his family's metal-construction shop in ruin, Ferrari and his widowed mother were on the brink of poverty. Enzo then charged after his third ambition within the auto and racing industry at age 21.

Ferrari was turned down from a position at Fiat before eventually joining the racing department at Alfa Romeo. There he helped Romeo build a successful racing team by winning some of the first postwar sporting events. He then lured a group of top engineers and talent from racing competitors to create his independent banner, a prancing horse in front of a yellow background, which would become Ferrari's legendary logo.

In his storied career as a race car driver, an auto engineer, a race team owner, and eventually the brand name of his company, Ferrari demanded *passion*, discipline, and results from everyone. Refusing to take vacations, he gave his workers regular tongue lashings to make sure they maintained the necessary fire to produce. He encouraged them just as strongly when they failed. And as his racing teams continued to win, Ferrari's exclusive, high-performance race cars became the envy of all adrenalin-inspired enthusiasts.

Like the Ferrari brand, the color red is imperative. We *must* choose red in order to seize the moment of opportunity! The alternative offers only mediocrity. And to exist without the choice of red is to risk the prospect of never experiencing the real invigoration and gift of life. So learn to fill up your *red paper cup* with all that you have to offer. The choice is all yours.

Red is what is meant by *passion, commitment, dedication, loyalty*, and *consistency*. These are The Five Elements of Love. *Love* is *passion*. And *passion* is red.

CHAPTER 5

PASSION

Webster's Third New International Dictionary defines the word *passion* as an intense feeling of emotion, or an individual who is overwhelmed by a state of excitement, surrendering to an uncontrollable and outward display. *Passion* is also explained as enthusiasm; a strong liking and or devotion to some activity, object, or concept.

Well, if you've ever wondered about some of the keys to the success of the super retail chain store of Wal-Mart, I had a chance in the winter of 2002 to view the company's rank and file of passionate managers up close and personal.

After I became a *New York Times* best-selling author in August 2000, Wal-Mart began to buy and sell a lot of my books in mass market softback. My title *Flyy Girl*, in particular, was outselling a number of other books in their fiction department. I was then invited to one of their national managers' meetings at the flagship location in Bentonville, Arkansas.

On an early Saturday morning in February 2002, I sat inside a bright Wal-Mart auditorium, packed with several hundred of their staff. As I listened to regional managers stand before the group and give testimonials of how they moved their individual stores over hurdles, through roadblocks, and around mine fields to reach their coveted sales goals for the quarter, I was impressed.

When you talk about intense emotion, enthusiasm, devotion, and outward displays of excitement, the Wal-Mart staff of managers had *passion* to spare. I thought that *I* was a good speaker and storyteller. But the Wal-Mart sales managers made me feel like an amateur. They had my undivided attention. Each successive sales story got better than the last, as if they were all out to top each other with humor, drama, cliffhangers, and climatic turns in the dark, all before they arrived at their successful sales goals. Once they finished their impassioned presentations for their fellow staff members, they received loud applause from the Wal-Mart faithful in the room.

It felt as though they could go on giving fired-up speeches for days. They had me feeling as if *I* wanted to work at Wal-Mart. *Let's go out and sell it all to the world!*

I then found myself praying that they wouldn't ask me to speak. I wasn't sure I could keep the same energy going. I felt I would only disappoint the crowd. Fortunately, they didn't ask the invited guests to add anything to their discussions. So I continued to listen to their speeches and make mental notes.

With many of us already aware of the overwhelming popularity of the Wal-Mart brand, we may now take the company's success for granted. We already know about their thousands of super stores, their low prices, their Walton family money, and many of us have heard plenty of news reports about the recent lawsuits filed against the company from past employees. Some of you are even tired of hearing about Wal-Mart.

Nevertheless, there are reasons why companies are successful that smart business people need to study. One of the most undervalued keys to the success of the Wal-Mart brand was right there in front me. With their thousands of worldwide staff members, the huge company continues to find passionate people to help run their everyday operations. How else could they manage such an expansive enterprise based on frugality? Simply put, enough people had to feel *passion* toward the company and its goals in order for it continue to grow and to remain profitable. And each time a new Wal-Mart super store opened, you could be assured that their bottom-line resource of devoted managers would be set in place to help run it.

Going back to the company founder, Sam Walton, there was no doubt the man was frugal. As legend has it, even after making his first billion in the 1980s, Walton continued to drive around Bentonville in a Ford pickup truck. In his earlier years of building the company in the 1950s, Walton set out to make everyone his friend, while convincing much of his staff to work overtime hours, barely at minimum wage. However, he sugarcoated his shrewd business practices by offering profit-sharing deals to his managers, and allowing his general staff to buy company stock at a discount. And if his employees could choose to share in the ownership of the company, then Walton could feel righteous about how hard he pushed them.

Decades later, Wal-Mart continues to drive a hard and passionate bargain through the devotion of its staff members. I found that they definitely know how to talk the talk, and based on their company track record, they know how to walk the walk. And until their company begins to use robots for customer service and operational management, their passionate staff members will remain a major part of their international success.

They had invited me out to share in the celebration of our combined accomplishments. Lesson learned, the trip to Bentonville served to reinforced my own *passion*, and taught me to respect the Wal-Mart motto; if you want your business to be successful, then act like you want it to be.

Regardless of Wal-Mart's dominant status within the retail industry, the obvious goal of the company is to remain excited, continue to grow, and continue to hire people who believe in their program.

The Wal-Mart brass makes it very clear that they will not back down. Nor should you. You should remain excited about your business goals no matter what. That's what having *passion* is all about. So as the old saying goes, 'You may hate 'em, but you gotta respect 'em."

Remaining excited about a progressive goal is the positive side of *passion*. On the negative side, *passion* can also lead to frustration, anger, and acts of violence. But like the color red, *passion* is the real deal; it cuts through the fallacies and brings out the truth.

What are you passionate about? If your answer is, "Nothing," or "I don't know," chances are that you are not on your way to personal success, or at least not until you find out what motivates you toward goals.

What is your *passion*? This is a fundamental but simple question. To respond with no answer is unacceptable. That's similar to refusing to breathe. You *have* to be passionate about *something*.

On the flip side of *The Equation*, successful businesses are also able to *evoke passion* from a consumer. What products or services are the people in your community passionate about supporting? What products of *passion* do you have to offer them?

Supplying the products of *passion* is another lesson of successful business. If you have no service or product to offer that anyone wants, and you cannot make people desire it, then you may want to reevaluate your enterprise.

A few years prior to making my decision to target a younger reading audience with my novels, I remember the dejection that I felt in the fall of 1998. I was on tour for a new book release entitled, *Single Mom*, depicting the contemporary struggle of U.S. families. Unfortunately, my book signing at a top-floor kiosk in the Pentagon City Mall in Alexandria, Virginia, happened to fall on the same day as the release of a new edition of John Madden's NFL Football video game from Sony Playstation.

I'm not suggesting here that a novel and a sports video game are within the same marketplace. However, the video game store was less than 15 feet in front from my book signing at the kiosk. And as I waited patiently to sell and sign my new book, with only a handful of customers interested in buying it, I couldn't help noticing the steady line of grown men who poured in and out the video store in front of me.

As soon as the video game line would go down, a new group of grown men would walk into the store and line up.

I stood there at the book store kiosk watching this with envy, and I began to shake my head next to the young male clerk who was on shift at the book store.

"So this game is really popular, huh?" I commented to the clerk. Smiling, he answered, "Yeah, it's the new John Madden."

The consumer *passion* for the new video game was obvious to him. But at 29 years old, I hadn't played video games in years. So the demographics disturbed me the most. The majority of guys buying this video game were older than I was, and yet they refused to even look at a book for sale. At that moment, I realized that I had to find a stronger product and a different audience who would be as passionate about my writing as these grown men were about John Madden's video football game.

When I later changed the focus of my material and the consumer audience that I targeted, the timely decision made all of the difference. I was then able to reach the *New York Times* bestseller's list for the first time in my writing career, which eventually led to my invitation to Wal-Mart.

A passionate response to services and products is what most businesses hope for. The goal is always to capture the attention of the masses. Why else would so many businesses advertise?

However, on both sides of the coin, as a business of *passion* that provides services and products, or a consumer of *passion* who buys them, the end result of having more *passion* then less, will usually lead to more business.

Passionate people are 100 percent people. They are the proven warriors, like Wal-Mart, who rarely back down from a worthwhile challenge. And they tend to be at peace with their *passion*, using their excitable energies to help them reach their goals.

A lack of effort is never the issue with a person or business of *passion*. To go all out is the norm. So on a scale of 1 to 20, with 1 being the least passionate and 20 being the most passionate, how would you honestly rate your ability to surrender to displays of excitement, have enthusiasm and devotion, or become overwhelmed by the career, products, services or company goals that you believe in?

The Passion Chart

Please Consider Your Most Honest Mark Below

1 - 2 - 3 - 4 - 5 - 6 - 7 - 8 - 9 - 10 - 11 - 12 - 13 - 14 - 15 - 16 - 17 - 18 - 19 - 20

The immediate issue with the validity and accuracy of such a chart is the number of variables that will ultimately change the answer, including the understanding of the definition of *passion*. We must also specify each particular goal or time period that we are referring to when we grade ourselves. Each and every one of us could have multiple goals and different years of assessment that would change our individual marks accordingly.

Time, experience, personal, and company history also change us. Some of us have goals that we were more passionate about a few years ago than we are now. Once those older goals have been achieved, abandoned, and or reevaluated, we usually redefine them or develop new ones. But are we as passionate about our new goals as we were about the old ones?

Sometimes, depending on our reevaluations and inspired awakenings in life, we become more passionate about our new goals. I wrote this book with the intention of reminding others of the goals that they have in mind to achieve.

Essentially, people or companies must evaluate their honest marks to their *present* (*job, career,* or *goal*), their *preferred* (*job, career,* or *goal*), and their *dream* (*job, career,* or *goal*), where applicable, and then note how the numbers change accordingly. We can also compare our marks to the *beginning* of our careers, the *peak* of our careers, and the *decline* of our careers, where applicable. And unless your goals have not been affected over time, the numbers will change accordingly, which will in turn affect the balance of the results. But before we can effectively utilize *The Equation* Chart, we must first understand the definitions, case studies, and discussions of all the needed components, colors, and elements within this text.

CHAPTER 6

COMMITMENT

The definition of *commitment* in *Webster's Third New International Dictionary* is the act of doing or performing. If we are not doing or performing something, then we are not going to get much done. Making a *commitment* to perform a certain task, to provide a certain services, or to create a certain product is where business begins.

The dictionary goes on to explain a *commitment* as an obligation or a pledge to carry out some policy or to give support to some policy or person. In short, a person gives her word to be accountable.

Accountability is a vital factor to any successful business or individual. Once you give your word, people expect you to honor it. Those who lack confidence in their ability to follow through are obviously not fast to commit. They would rather just play things by ear, as we often like to say.

Running your business in a random style with hit-or-miss execution creates difficulties in establishing track records and inspiring trust in potential customers or clients. People do not wants to play things by ear when their investment is on the line. They want to know what they are getting themselves into. Most individuals will not engage in any serious or long-term agreement without the assurance of a *commitment* first.

What I've noticed in my interactions with aspiring entrepreneurs is that many people think less about the *commitment* of their business offering, and more about the dream of becoming wealthy. But dreams without *commitment* will often get a dreamer brushed aside in the execution of real business. Real business is about making a *commitment* to achieve one specific goal at a time and getting that goal done.

That's what *commitment* is all about. But in the get-rich-as-quick-as-you-can world, where people jump onto whatever boat they feel they need to climb aboard to succeed, fewer people are willing to stick to the plans they need to carry out in order to *earn* that success.

In higher education, the four years or more that it takes to graduate from most universities is about *commitment* as well. Companies want to know if you are willing to do what it takes to graduate from an institution after completing various projects and assignments over a number of years.

Interns and apprenticeships are other forms of *commitment*. Are you willing to work for free or for less than minimum wage, while you learn the professional skills and structure of a particular trade or business? Many people answer no. They believe their time and effort are too important to work for free or for a much lower income than they feel they are worth. So they seek other positions of employment where there is less of a *commitment* to learn the applied skill that they need to perform.

However, if you settle for no *commitment* in your craft in life, as the survivalists often do, then you will receive no *commitment* from your employer. And just as they can hire you easily, they can also fire you easily. You don't owe them much, and they don't owe you much.

No smart corporation is willing to pay for employees to learn a higher-skill position unless they have already *earned* that opportunity for themselves through a strong track record. They are then asked to make a *commitment* to enlighten the company through the use of their higher degree of skills. So all men and women must commit themselves to learn what they need to learn over time, prove that they've learned it, and then interview for the higher position with their track record in order. That is how a *commitment* pays off. You have to "pay the cost to be the boss."

The element of *commitment* is also necessary for a company to succeed. Take for example the *commitment* that Jeff Bezos made in 1995 when he decided to create an online service for book sales through the creation of Amazon.com.

Like many of us who start our own companies, Bezos collected investments from the familiar sources of family and friends before launching his start-up in Seattle, Washington. But who would ever think that something as mundane as selling books online would ever become the juggernaut of success that Amazon.com represents today?

Well, it all starts with a *commitment*. Bezos has remained committed to figuring out ways to make it work, while remaining competitive. He first evaluated what his online customers would want. His research came up with good books, good prices, and a fast and cheap delivery. So the committed entrepreneur went about supplying what his customers wanted.

Based on their online ratings system of book orders and fan reviews, Amazon.com bought up boxes of books at the lowest prices by buying them in bulk and then storing them in ready-to-ship warehouses. As business began to take off in the late 1990s, Amazon's online customers were so pleased with Bezos's *commitment* to serving their needs that they began to ask for other items that could be ordered online. Amazon responded by expand its selection of goods and making sure that they were stocked.

The next thing we knew, Bezos's committed company began to save the day for thousands of parents on Christmas when retail stores and company web sites would run out of stock of the hottest new toys. The national media coverage of Amazon's heroic feats became golden. And then the competitors came.

Hundreds of new companies with bright ideas figured they could all sell items online and become as successful as Amazon overnight. However, many of these new start-ups, and the investors who backed them, were much more committed to making money than to providing sincere services. So instead working out the kinks of their businesses over time, as Bezos had done with Amazon, these new dot-coms frustrated thousands of customers who attempted to use them, before the public eventually decided to ignore them.

At the break of the millennium, the dot-com industry began to look dire as hundreds of unsuccessful companies wasted billions of dollars in start-up capital. It was assumed that Amazon.com, as one of the leaders of the online retail industry, would crash and burn as well. Nevertheless, Bezos's company continued to grow, while serving its customer needs as usual. Through steady reserve and focus, Amazon.com increased its business, expanding shipments and warehouses internationally.

Bezos's staunch *commitment* to customer service had obviously paid off, and the public felt secure with his brand. Amazon.com had established a proven model, and had gained accountability, recognition, and customer loyalty. As a result, Jeff Bezos became one of the fastest self-made billionaires on the planet. But instead of taking his new wealth, selling his company, and running to something else, Bezos continues to reinvest in Amazon, with more committed goals for the company's future.

How many of us are that committed to achieve our goals and to stand strong on the principles that we believe in? The most powerful *commitment* we could ever make is to ourselves, to do what we say we plan to do.

Successful individuals make the most important pledge to themselves, to be as thorough as they can before they commit to anyone else. So when they finally do make a long-term *commitment* in industry, their pledge is indeed valuable, by first making themselves and their services valuable. This is the Amazon example. The company remains successful by remaining committed to service.

The dictionary completes the definition of *commitment* by calling it a state of being obligated or bound by making a decisive, or a moral choice that involves a person in a definite course of action.

This "definite course of action" is also known as focus. Committed people have a definite and focused goal in mind that outside forces cannot derail. Extremely focused individuals spend as much time and labor over as many details as possible to ensure that the job is done correctly. In doing so, they usually develop new, more effective techniques and strategies. These achievements increase the confidence that develops poise. And once an individual develops poise on the job, he or she becomes unflappable and can commit to much higher goals for themselves and or for the company.

As in the example of Amazon.com, committed people are able to see the big picture and design their goals accordingly. And as the noncommitted employee carefully watches the clock for quitting time, the committed man or woman works harder on the product for more effective execution.

So on a scale of 1 to 20, with 1 being the least committed and 20 being the most committed, how would you honestly rate your pledge to follow through on your personal or professional goals, with or without compensation, while obligated to a moral choice and a definite course of action in your career or company?

The Commitment Chart
Please Consider Your Most Honest Mark Below

1 - 2 - 3 - 4 - 5 - 6 - 7 - 8 - 9 - 10 - 11 - 12 - 13 - 14 - 15 - 16 - 17 - 18 - 19 - 20

It is a stronger moral choice to make a *commitment* to the things that we truly *love*, believe in and feel *passion* for than to be swayed by that which is faster, easier, or deemed more lucrative at the moment. Being hired to perform at face value typically means that there is no expected upside to your abilities. However, making a strong *commitment*, while receiving no or minimum wage, or even wages through commission, will eventually pay off in added professional reserve and experience that is invaluable. In the long run, we will each learn our own lessons as to why. But for the sake of our personal growth and progress in business, we must all be honest with our present marks of *commitment*. If you find yourself jumping from one thing to the next, and rarely standing ground on what you believe is the correct life and career path to follow, then you may need to question what your real goals are and add some iron to your character.

Consult the final section, "The Equation in Use," for more details.

CHAPTER 7

DEDICATION

The definition of *dedication* in *Webster's Third New International Dictionary* is devoting or setting aside for any particular purpose; an appropriation or giving up of property to public use that precludes the owner or others claiming under him from asserting any right of ownership inconsistent with the use for which the property is dedicated.

To simplify its definition, *dedication* is basically the setting aside of time, effort, creativity, land, capital, or resources for a specific person, group, or purpose that is to be maintained for that particular purpose. In other words, you agree to dedicate yourself to any and all efforts that are necessary to achieve a particular goal, principle, or idea and nothing else.

The old adage, "practice makes perfect" sums up the importance of *dedication* in achieving one's goals, or at least moves one closer toward them. To practice is to dedicate time for strategy and training that eventually help you to perform better at your career task.

Andrew Cherng, company founder and chairman of Panda Restaurant Group, is so sincere about his *dedication* and practice of hiring managers and staff, who share in his spiritual values that he has turned down billions in projected revenue his company could earn by selling thousands of new franchises of Panda Express.

Cherng, an American immigrant born in Yangzhou, China, would rather maintain his practice of inquiring about the well-being, personal lives, hobbies, spiritual beliefs, and relationships of his managers and employees. He fears that independent franchise owners could not be trusted to continue the work of personal and spiritual enlightenment that he believes is the key to the success of his chain of restaurants.

A math major at Baker University in Baldwin City, Kansas, Cherng met his wife and business partner, Peggy, in college. In 1970, after graduation, the young couple moved to Los Angeles. Andrew then took a job managing his cousin's Hunan restaurant, while his wife worked as a computer programmer.

In 1973, Cherng pulled together $60,000 from friends and family to open his own restaurant, Panda Inn, and hired his father to run the kitchen. After five years of *dedication* to spirituality, family, and business—in that order—Cherng was asked to adapt his family-run Panda Inn menu for the food court at a new mall location in Glendale, California. Five years later, in 1983, Panda Express had expanded with stores in 13 more locations.

However, Cherng had remained dedicated to his personal and spiritual practice of meditation, self-improvement, and human balance, while hiring and training all of his company employees. As the company continued to grow, expanding to more than a thousand locations in 36 states, Cherng spent years away from his wife and three daughters, causing a strain in the balance of his own personal life.

Nevertheless, with 75 percent ownership of a near billion dollar company, the founder refuses to let go of his value system. He now leads monthly personal wellness seminars for hundreds of his staff members to hear about nutrition, intimacy, and self-awareness. He encourages his store managers to practice the same with their staff members. He also encourages participation in community charities, education, effective parenting, and the joy of hobbies. To ease the pressures on his marriage, Cherng convinced his wife Peggy to hire an operations boss to help them run the company.

Convinced that *dedication* to his company's spiritual values is more important than the money it earns, Cherng has fired skilled employees who have repeatedly failed his personal commitment tests. The company founder is that earnest about the overall balance in his employee's lives.

For those who accept and share in his beliefs of the company's success through greater spiritual purpose, his Panda Restaurant Group has rewarded managers with a 20 percent share of annual sales growth at their stores, reaching up to $50,000 on top of their base salary, which can range from $35,000 to $63,000. For employees who log at least 30-hour work weeks, the company gives them full health benefits.

Remarkably, despite the strict enforcement of Cherng's dedicated principles, manager turnover at Panda Express is at *half* the restaurant industry average, with only one company lawsuit in 2003, which Panda won in court.

Now that's *dedication!* We should all think about Cherng's level of serious practice when evaluating the career principles that we believe in for our own companies.

But how many of you would honestly leave billions of dollars on the table because of a conflict in your principles? However, Andrew Cherng holds firmly to the T. Harv Eker adage: "The way you do anything is the way you do everything," from the bestselling book, *Secrets of the Millionaire Mind* (2005). And with more than a thousand restaurants that continue to grow at new shopping mall locations, while still gaining in revenue, Cherng's *dedication* to spiritual practice has obviously been successful.

In my own career, I dedicated myself to becoming a writer like a fish to water. Once I transferred to Howard University and changed my major from Pharmacy to Print Journalism, instead of procrastinating, or waiting around for stories to write, the plight of far too many journalism majors, I decided to create my own writing assignments. And I became published in the student newspapers immediately. I then became a sports writer for the student-run *Community News*, publishing articles on youth sports in the Washington, DC, area.

I moved on to a summer internship with the local press of Washington, DC, after my junior year, where I engaged in my first career job interview with Barry Murray, a 38-year-old editor, who was also a co-owner at *The Capital Spotlight* newspaper. I gave him my sample of 10 published articles from Howard, and he sat back in his editor's chair and looked up at me.

The first thing I thought was that I probably needed more experience. But he could see my *dedication* to the craft of writing from the first few minutes of getting to know each other. He told me that other interns hadn't bothered to write anything before asking for a position. So I already had a leg up on the competition.

Well, Mr. Murray gave me the internship, and not only did I write articles for the local press that summer, I wrote and published front page stories of major political, educational, health, sports, and crime news in the nation's capital before my senior year of college. I would show up at local news events at the tender age of 21, with my own business cards and a recognizable byline, and veteran journalists were stunned. *Who is this young college student writing major articles?* It was a great feeling.

By the time I entered my senior year of school, I was practically a professional writer already. Then I came up with the idea to write my own column for *The Hilltop*, the major Howard University paper. I called my column "Food For Thought," and I had Charles Ford, the lead cameramen at *The Capital Spotlight* take a picture of me in a professional sweater and tie, while holding a sharpened pencil in hand.

I wrote two sample articles and submitted them with my photo to George Daniels, the senior editor at *The Hilltop* that semester, and he loved the column idea. We had been in a few classes together, and he had followed my work with *The Capital Spotlight*. But I had no idea how big that first column in *The Hilltop* would be.

I wrote about the Supreme Court selection of Clarence Thomas, and my photo was included with the column heading, twice as large as I expected it to be. I viewed my first "Food For Thought" article and was shocked. I was nervous about it, but in a good way. And my column became the spotlight of the commentary page.

After the first "Food For Thought" article was published to great response, the student editors at *The Hilltop* all agreed to continue to run my column each week, but with one exception. They informed me that they would have to make space for other students to write columns as well. In all fairness, they wanted to create a balance of opportunities for the other writers.

However, as I continued to write and publish new articles, week after week, it became obvious that I was the only student writer dedicated enough to have a column. Writing a column *needs dedication.* You can't write a great article one week and then disappear from the publication the next. Readers begin to expect your regular input. But there were barely three articles published from the other student columnists that semester.

I went on to publish 13 consecutive "Food For Thought" articles, and became one of the most consistent and celebrated student writers at school. I had a solid readership on campus, as well as in the city of Washington, DC. And I was not being paid a dime yet for my time or my efforts.

Eighteen years later, I continue to dedicate myself to read, write, think, and learn about new subjects that I may eventually utilize for books, articles, films, lectures, or talks in the future. And if you consider yourself to be involved in a career that you're serious about, then practice and *dedication* should definitely be a part of your mantra.

Even as a young college student, I was as adamant about my career as a writer as Andrew Cherng has been about the spirituality of his employees at Panda Express restaurants. You will find that more successful people than not are strict followers of dedicated practice and belief in their work. But if you are not willing to set aside the necessary time, effort, and resources to practice the elements of your craft, then why should you expect to become successful at it?

On a scale of 1 to 20, with 1 being the least dedicated and 20 being the most dedicated, how would you honestly rate your ability to sacrifice personal time, effort, creativity, land, or capital for the attainment of the individual or group goals in the career that you have?

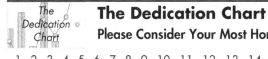

The Dedication Chart

Please Consider Your Most Honest Mark Below

1 - 2 - 3 - 4 - 5 - 6 - 7 - 8 - 9 - 10 - 11 - 12 - 13 - 14 - 15 - 16 - 17 - 18 - 19 – 20

Dedication is easier to attain when you have *passion* and *commitment* for a particular purpose. When that purpose is wrapped in something you really *love*, *dedication* makes perfect sense. However, it makes a lot less sense to dedicate yourself to goals that you barely care about. The math of *dedication* is that simple.

CHAPTER 8

LOYALTY

Loyalty, as defined by *Webster's Third New International Dictionary*, is the quality, state or instance of being loyal; faithful and unswerving in allegiance. Through both fostering and practicing *loyalty*, companies, teams, organizations, and individuals cultivate stability in business and in life. More often than not, this precious element is based more on character than on price. *Loyalty* is hard to earn and not easily bought.

Earning the *loyalty* of others is a goal to be worked towards diligently, like the *loyalty* of millions of Internet customers who use Google, a billion-dollar Internet search engine that I have never seen advertised outside of my computer screen.

I can't recall when I first heard the word "Google" used in a sentence. The term just seemed to drop out of the sky. It seemed as though everyone started using it at the same time.

The concept itself was ingenious. Anything that you searched for online could be found through this tool. The researched item only needed to be listed, like the Yellow Pages. But what so many customers loyal to Google appreciated was that the search engine actually worked quicker and more effectively than any other resource. It was a quality service that people were more than happy to promote through word of mouth. And the *loyalty* of its initial customers quickly influenced the *loyalty* of others.

The viral idea, to allow the search engine to spread online was thought up and maintained by Google founder's, Larry Page and Sergey Brin. The duo were just a couple of Stanford University students who decided to develop a way to organize the world's information and make it universally accessible and useful to all who bothered.

Starting out in Brin's dorm room, the Stanford under grads utilized the mathematical principles of "Beyond the Googol," as noted in the book *Mathematics and the Imagination* (2001), by Edward Kasner and James Newman, to eventually outdo Yahoo! and Netscape, two of the dominant search engines at the time.

Who could ever forget the popular Yahoo! commercials that screamed out the company name like a yodeling, computer cowboy; "YA-HOOOOO-UUUUU!"

Nevertheless, Brin and Page were able to come up with a more efficient system of web page and general information search rankings based on counting the amount of extended link pages to each search. In other words, the more extended links that could be found for a certain company, name, or web site, the higher the ranking he, she, or it would receive, moving the site to the top of the search page. The system was lightning fast, orderly, and fully comprehensible. And before long, everyone at Stanford was using it.

Once the search engine idea extended outside of the Stanford network, Brin and Page decided to continue its organic, or viral, word-of-mouth marketing instead of paying for expensive advertising campaigns. If the idea could work for college students, then why not for the general public? And boy did they strike it rich with that idea!

Companies began to gain millions of new customers by being found, and the Google search engine that helped them to do so was not even boasting about it. Who's not going to be loyal to that? Having your brand name, products, and services discovered and researched by the public is crucial. As the people, places, companies, and things continued to list themselves online, Google's satisfied and loyal base of customers began to skyrocket.

The Google company's savvy of creating organically earned *loyalty* became a gold mine. With the company engine of Google just popping and happening to us, the public had no way of forming a real opinion about it. You just did it; you "googled." And you did it again and again until the company name had established itself as an Internet verb, leaving Yahoo! in the dust, as its loud, yodeling commercials became dated and irritating.

Brin and Page held strong to their philosophy of not clobbering customers over the head every five minutes with why you should use them. The Google network became user friendly, as if they were not a company of profits. By remaining loyal to their own business principles, the Stanford duo maintained a university-like innocence that extended to their staff members, and made them feel comfortable, important, and respected.

The Google way of enhancing *loyalty* was a real rarity in the new millennium corporate culture of outsourcing work, while minimalizing and downsizing the little guy. In less than a decade, with the help of investments from venture capitalists, glowing media coverage, continued widespread use, and professional corporate leadership all jumping on board, the Google organization exploded, creating a new industry of young, multi-millionaires, who had succeeded outside of the normal corporate structure.

Knowing that loyal employees would be the key to sustaining long-term success, the innovators behind Google knew they would have to work double-time to focus on employee retention. Today, Google features one of the most impressive lists of employee benefits. From free, healthy meals prepared by gourmet chefs to shuttle service to an on-site doctor, Google continues to inspire company *loyalty* from within.

With Eric Schmidt as Google's present CEO, the company's ultimate goal is to strip away the stress of corporate hierarchy and/or personal issues that may impede employees from achieving professionalism and progress. The company provides a standard package of fringe benefits, with dining facilities, gyms, laundry rooms, massage rooms, haircuts, carwashes, dry cleaning, commuting buses, and a general first-class treatment that is available to all of their hardworking engineers. Included in employee perks is a Google Founder's Award, higher salaries for new employees, and opportunities for participation in the company's equity and growth, which allows employees to increase their personal salaries through the success of the overall company.

Google's strong example of *loyalty*, both within and outside of their corporate offices, is a perfect case study of how a company builds the fabric, trust, and longevity of employees and customers alike, while giving a business added strength from which to prosper. Loyal individuals and organizations have not only found ways of handsomely compensating their staff, teammates, managers, and the supportive community around them, but they have also shown respect through compassion, tact and fairness, where even disagreements are handled with care and professionalism.

The term *brand loyalty* is a often used to describe the members of a consumer community who consistently show support of a particular company or product, like the *loyalty* I have to the Ford Motor Company. They were the first to offer me a fair percentage car loan of 12.5 percent before I had any real credit under my belt. I had initially walked away from the Honda, Toyota, and Mazda dealerships for trying to get me to pay more than 15 percent on a car loan. At the time, in the early 1990s, foreign car dealerships were the leaders in the market on entry-level vehicles, and many of their dealerships saw no need to work with a recent college grad who had no credit history.

The Ford Motor Company took a chance at offering me a fair opportunity to prove myself at 12.5 percent, which was still a point higher than what I begged for. However, the Ford finance officer put it to me convincingly, I had to start my credit history with something, and then I could improve it from there.

So I took a deep breath and decided to fork over a hard-earned, and saved, $4,000 as a down payment to keep my monthly car note low. And it was money well spent. I drove away from the Ford dealership with my first financed car in the spring of 1994, a shiny, two-door, turquoise Ford Probe. It was a brand-new Ford model, with rounded curves like a Jaguar.

The Ford Probe had a hatchback with enough trunk space to load ten boxes of books inside (roughly 500 units) with the back seats folded down. I then drove the car on business trips up and down Interstate 95, to Virginia, Baltimore, Philadelphia, New York, and New Jersey, where I collected anywhere from $600 to $2,400 per book run. In just a year and a half, I had racked up more than 80,000 road miles and collected close to a hundred thousand dollars in my sporty new vehicle, along with a half a dozen speeding tickets, mostly received in the state of Maryland. My wife then became pregnant with our first son and told me to trade my Probe in for a Ford Explorer. She could no longer bend down to climb into the car, nor did she look forward to the struggle of climbing back out of it.

Well, I went on to remain with the Ford family for five vehicles and 14 years, including two buys and three leases. I've even financed a XKR Jaguar sports car through Ford's ownership of the company in 2001, a car that I might never have been interested in if it were not for the fun I had while driving the Ford Probe. I was more of a big car man that a sports car man. Nevertheless, the opportunity to own a brand new sports car in my twenties gave me a chance to appreciate it, which led to my investment in another one.

My *loyalty* with Ford was established through a fair opportunity. The company allowed me the chance to prove myself, which led to some great years of business and family security through use of brand new vehicles that I could count on and finance, while building up my credit history. In return, I have practiced a history of giving *loyalty* to those individuals, family members, friends and or companies who have given me a fair shake at providing business.

Loyalty is a priceless means of nurturing and maintaining customer relations, staff, partners, teammates, and community support in any business. But one must be willing to do the things that build *loyalty* in the first place, as well as return *loyalty* when it has been earned. So using the examples of Ford and Google, how do you to cultivate *loyalty* in your business?

On a scale of 1 to 20, with 1 being the least loyal and 20 being the most loyal, how would you rate your ability to remain faithful and unswerving in allegiance? How would you rate your fidelity or tenacious adherence to the government, principles, or practices of your goal? How much are you willing to agree with a company platform or program in regard to your career? And how would you rate your ability to maintain that *loyalty* through good times and bad?

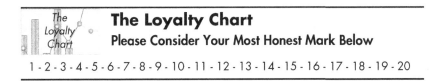

The Loyalty Chart
Please Consider Your Most Honest Mark Below

1 - 2 - 3 - 4 - 5 - 6 - 7 - 8 - 9 - 10 - 11 - 12 - 13 - 14 - 15 - 16 - 17 - 18 - 19 - 20

Loyalty toward an individual, goal, group, practice, brand, product or career is best attained when one feels *passion, commitment, dedication* and *love* in the treatment, quality, character, strength or availability of that given object. But if there is no reason to be loyal, then why give *loyalty*?

No one is loyal *just because*. There is always an explainable reason and history behind a person's, group's, or company's *loyalty* or disloyalty. All we need to do is investigate to figure out those answers. Then we can establish how to create consistent *loyalty* of our own.

CHAPTER 9

CONSISTENCY

Consistency, the final element of *love*, is defined in *Webster's Third New International Dictionary* as the condition of standing together or remaining fixed in union. It is the element that we all expect to be able to count on in business. *Consistency* is secured execution over a long period of time. And when people illustrate *consistency* in their specific field of work, we generally find ourselves expecting those individuals to perform reliably and successfully.

Consistency is what true stars are made of. They are able to reach a peak performance and maintain it. They are often victorious under pressure, and many of them have learned to feel at ease with the weight of the team or corporation on their shoulders.

Microsoft cofounder Bill Gates has been used to that kind of pressure since the early 1980s, when he and his business partner, Steven Ballmer, began talks on a history-making deal with IBM, who at the time, were the kings of the computer industry. Gates, never known as a man to don a great-looking suit, was a mere 24 years old, and looked even younger. He and Ballmer showed up in Florida to discuss the business of developing an operating system for IBM's first personal computer, and were accordingly grilled by the suit-and-tie establishment.

IBM's plan was to have Gates, a young computer whiz kid and Harvard University dropout, help them to develop their first personal computers for the mass market. The idea was to establish the PC as what it would become today, the private usable offices of high-tech civilization.

Gates had already established himself in high-tech circles as the codeveloper of the software to run Altair 8800, known as the first personal computer. He had developed the system with his friend and Microsoft cofounder, Paul Allen, a college dropout himself, from Washington State University. But these men were not college dropouts because they couldn't make the grades; they simply wanted a head start in the computer industry, before everyone else could catch up to them.

When IBM wanted to rush its PC to the market in less than a year, using off-the-shelf materials that were available to anyone, Bill Gates saw a golden opportunity for his own company's future. Using what he had already learned as a whiz kid, Gates figured out a consistent approach to stay ahead of the competition.

Instead of focusing on the IBM hardware computer, since IBM was less interested in developing the system that ran the computer, Gates took ownership of the rights to the system. Gates understood from his early partnership and conversations with Paul Allen, that plenty of get-rich-quick competitors would jump on board the computer industry ride before IBM knew what hit them. And in an arena of a thousand companies all rushing to make PCs for profit, Gates understood that they would all need software to run their programs, an ingenious assessment.

To jump in ahead of the game was why Gates and Allen had dropped out of college in the first place. Now they had found a golden opportunity not only to remain in front of the pack, but to dictate the terms of the competition. Gates then became a consistent master of creating, predicting, and securing as many new programs, software, and technology that he felt were needed to control the computer industry marketplace.

Continuing with his *consistency* of staying ahead of the competition, Gates also realized that competitors could entice any and every upcoming talent to defect from his rising empire to join their companies. So instead of placing his Microsoft headquarters smack down in the popular Silicon Valley area near San Francisco, Gates set up shop closer to home near Seattle, Washington, in an isolated area of Redmond. And in Redmond, he could recruit top-notch talent from around the world and have them create without worrying about rival companies trying to steal his best engineers. In other words, Gates had learned to plan for an advanced game of corporate chess, predicting all of the right moves within the industry.

The rest of the Bill Gates story became history. Microsoft went on to control a large share of the computer marketplace, making Gates a billionaire and a consistent name on the Forbes 400 list for 21 straight years, peaking in 1999, with a staggering personal wealth of $85 billion.

Microsoft is now listed at double the market value of IBM.

Taking a page out of Bill Gates's legendary book of consistent approach, whenever a business can be first, unique, aggressive, tactical, and consistent, it can establish itself ahead of the competition in any industry. What are your consistent strengths or the strengths of your company?

Consistency is also defined as persistence of firmness or single-ness of purpose in which a cheerful mood is maintained. This cheerful mood, as the dictionary explains it, is often referred to as being calm and cool under pressure, or simply being professional, getting the job done without worry.

In my own career as a writer, I remained consistent by thinking far in advance of what subjects I wanted to write about. My exe-cution was based mostly on what I felt were the most interesting current affairs of the day. I would then outline novel ideas that were based on those subjects accordingly. So as long as there was something of intrigue going on within the national community, I would never have a lack of subjects to write about.

I rarely waited around for stories to inspire me, as I heard other writers claim to do. I viewed inspiration as more of a tangible good that was all around me and not something supernatural that had to strike me over the head with lightning before I could write a good story. So I continued to write on deadline, publishing a new novel every summer, like clockwork, for 16 straight years.

But we must all understand that *consistency* happens first in the mind. Consistent people will produce the expected result mentally, before they ever perform or create it. The success of the work then becomes natural, when consistent individuals hold firm in their objective to see their ambitious ideas carried out to completion, again and again.

We may all be able to perform well enough to meet our goals once or twice, but *consistency* is being able to perform up to expectations all the time, like the consistent entrepreneur, brand maker, trendsetter, and past CEO of Def Jam Records, Shawn Corey Carter, better known as the rap star Jay-Z.

Carter climbed from the Marcy Project homes in Brooklyn, New York, as a sometime music DJ, to a recognized performer, tour headliner, number one lyricist, multiplatinum record award winner, clothing line maker of Rocawear, designer shoe endorser with Reebok, premier liquor owner of Armadale—a Scottish vodka brand-promoter with Anheuser-Busch, co-owner of the New Jersey Nets basketball franchise, night club owner of the 40/40 Clubs in Manhattan, Atlantic City, and Las Vegas, and is now recognized as a living legend and icon of American pop culture.

Year after year, Shawn Carter has found new ways to seize and hold America's attention through entrepreneurship and brand marketing, including his recent marriage to pop icon wife, Beyoncé Knowles.

After continuing an ongoing record of nine straight number one album releases in 13 years, Jay-Z has earned his status, and recently signed a $150 million deal with the Live Nation tour and promotions company to continue his success with record sales and concerts worldwide. The recent deal with Live Nation is reported to be amongst the most expensive contracts ever awarded to a musician. That's the meaning of *consistency* in business— continuing to create new opportunities from a solid and recognizable brand.

The final definition of *consistency* is an agreement or harmony of parts, traits, or features. *Harmony* is a word that implies that a certain musical balance is involved, where *consistency* evolves into a sense of rhythm, as in a left-right swing of a pendulum. In that regard, *consistency* becomes hypnotic and addictive, producing a craving from the audience, company members, teammates, or peers.

Consistency can then influence teammates, company members, or peers to become more consistent in their own performance, creating company or team inspiration. These inspirational individuals, often identified as The One, and to be further explained within the upcoming Gold Section, create an incredible amount of momentum that becomes motivating for not only the company, but for the business community as a whole.

How many of us have been passionate or successful in our own consistent efforts to reach a benchmark of inspiration in business for our community? How many of us have been a partner in business, or a member of a team or company with such an individual or a consistency of performance as a group?

There is a need for consistent individuals to surround themselves with others, who will be just as consistent in order to run a well-oiled machine. One man or woman cannot successfully execute a plan alone, no matter how consistent. There must be equilibrium, where the other parts of the machine collaborate on a common goal. The give and take of ideas becomes the normal execution, increasing the overall awareness of success in everyone. And in that consistent environment, every individual member learns to step up to the plate and do his part whenever needed.

Being prepared and able to perform consistently is an essential part of loving anything. To have *love* with *consistency* should be the career aspiration and goal of any individual, group, or company.

Love expects an individual to give her all. *Passion* expects her to be excited by it. A *commitment* is a bond that the individual pledges to contribute. *Dedication* is setting aside the time, effort, and principles needed to perform successfully. *Loyalty* is created by a person or company willing to stand by the team concept. And when we perform all these elements with *consistency*, a creation of *love* is the result.

To have all of The Five Elements of *love* in abundance is a great start toward success. On a scale of 1 to 20, with 1 being the least consistent and 20 being the most consistent, how would you honestly rate your ability to remain fixed at a high level of performance, while having persistence of firmness or singleness in purpose for yourself, a persistence that is also in harmony with your company, team, or organization in your career?

The Consistency Chart
Please Consider Your Most Honest Mark Below

1 - 2 - 3 - 4 - 5 - 6 - 7 - 8 - 9 - 10 - 11 - 12 - 13 - 14 - 15 - 16 - 17 - 18 - 19 - 20

We can now add up all of our marks from each element of *love*, and figure out the honest *numerator* scores of our *present, preferred* and *dream job, career* or *goal*, in the final section, "The Equation in Use," as we move on to the component, color and elements of *art*.

ART IS COMPETITIVE

L/A*S=B L/A*S=B L/A*S=B L/A*S=
L/A*S=B L/A*S=B L/A*S=B L/A*S=B
L/A*S=B L/A*S=B L/A*S=B L/A*S=
CHAPTER 10
L/A*S=B L/A*S=B L/A*S=B L/A*S=B
L/A*S=B L/A*S=B L/A*S=B L/A*S=

THE DEFINITION OF ART

Now that we've defined the The Five Elements of *love* and determined our personal or company's *numerator score*, we move on to define what is meant by the term *art*, and The Five Elements that comprise it, to determine our personal or company's *denominator score*.

Art, the second indisputable component of *The Equation*, is indicated by the color gold and symbolized by a *pyramid*. As the elements of *love* fill up an inexpensive *paper cup* to 100 percent capacity, inversely, the elements of *art* have the singular and hard-earned goal of becoming #1 at the top of a complicated and competitive rise of a *pyramid*. The goal of *art* is to become individually recognizable through quality.

Webster's Third New International Dictionary defines *art* as the power of performing certain actions, especially as acquired by experience, study, or observation. The dictionary explains that *art* is skill in the adaptation of things in the natural world for the uses of human life. *Art* is a branch of learning, an occupation or business requiring knowledge or skill of a certain craft. It is also the systematic application of that skill.

The important questions for the component of *art* then becomes, How skilled are we at performing the objects of our pursuits? Are we skilled enough to attain our goals within a given field? And if that given field is crowded with competitors, does our particular level of skill allow us to compete successfully enough to find our own niche of supporters? What is it that makes our products or services desirable? And are we ready to compete at performing our specified *art* to establish their value within the business community?

With this second component of *The Equation*, your personal or company art will be evaluated by a certain rank whether you like it or not. Within any professional field, people have natural tendencies to compare products and services, particularly in terms of price value or an evaluation of fair compensation. Both individual customers and private companies will make judgment calls on who is qualified to best serve their needs. And if your skills are not honed enough to be deemed valuable, then you may find yourself left out of business opportunities until you are able to improve your expertise.

The reality is that we can all *love* what we do 100 percent, but if that *love* does not ultimately produce a stronger level of *art*, we may need to refocus our profession toward a field where we are more competitive.

Realizing that many of us may choose to provide the same services or products within a given community, one must eventually accept the fact that the value of the *art* will be determined by the acknowledged skill of the artist. To honestly rank ourselves, we must take our skills and the skills of others into professional consideration. We must ask ourselves, *"What are the elements of my craft that make me more or less valuable and competitive? And how do I correctly assess those elements to strengthen or modify my skills to compete?"*

Even to find a job with a company, one must qualify with skills that are needed to perform certain positions. A supervisor position will need more applicable skill than an entry position. A managerial position will need more applicable skill than a supervisor position. A vice president position will need more applicable skill than a managerial position. And the #1 position, the CEO of the company, will need more skills than anyone.

The company CEO must perform up to par and be competitive in his or her *art, period*. There is no way around it. The position of company leadership must set the course to perform the necessary tasks that move the company forward. Otherwise, the company could become a car with no engine. There is no forward movement.

In an essay published in *Entrepreneur* magazine, Robert Kiyosaki, bestselling author of the *Rich Dad, Poor Dad* series of books, noted that successful business leaders have the drive and tenacity to be the best. And they prepare themselves to win.

Explaining four types of business personalities, Kiyosaki discussed those who worked to be liked, those who work to be comfortable, those who work to be right, and those who work to win. Within a business structure, all four personality types are needed, but one type must be concerned about the bottom line of competition in their field of work in order for the company to be successful. Someone has to ask the question, *"How do we become good enough to compete?"*

Kiyosaki explained that those who worked to be liked are great as social directors, who desire for the team to be happy, and are good with personnel, but that they often shy away from conflict or stating what needs to be said or done to perform. Those who work to be comfortable enjoy job security and will generally perform well, as long as they are not forced to perform under pressure or stress, or under tough deadlines. Those who work to be right, who are often specialized professionals, have had the disadvantage of a reluctance to consider other points of views. But those who work to win will strive at nothing less than the goal of moving themselves and the company forward. These leaders are ready and willing to utilize all resources of the team to make sure that the bottom line of success is met.

Roger Shiffman, cofounder of Tiger Electronics toy company, had a *love* for toys and electronics when he began his company in 1978. But he was also well abreast of the bottom line for competing against other toy manufacturers for business. With prior experience in the retail toy industry, Shiffman worked at a wholesaler in his teen years, just as electronic games were being embraced by the masses.

Excited by the prospect of getting involved in the electronic toy industry as a product creator and manufacturer himself, shortly after graduating from college, Shiffman launched his own electronics toy brand with Tiger, where he developed handheld games. His *art* of innovative toy making was solidified with the creation of Furby, a high-tech, electronic, furry pet that talked, and ignited a public sensation. In three years, Tiger Electronics sold more than 41 million units of Furby, becoming one of the fastest-growing and successful toy brands in the industry.

After selling his Tiger Electronics company to the toy giant of Hasbro in 1998 for a respectable $335 million, Shiffman found himself reinspired to compete in the *art* of toy making in 2002, forming the Zizzle brand with Marc Rosenberg, one of his past executives and friends from Tiger.

Known in the toy industry as a veteran and competitive businessman, in a newly crowded field, Shiffman decided to compete this time in the action figure department. Defusing the doubts of his management team at the newly formed Zizzle, who were more familiar with the creation of electronic toys, Shiffman had them zero in on the most robust retail categories, finding that action figures did incredibly well within the industry. His new start-up company then went on to win the rights to produce toys based on the movie *Pirates of the Caribbean* in 2005, a deal estimated at worth $100 million a year.

To stay competitive in the toy market against the giants of Hasbro and Mattel, as well as keeping tabs on the lightning-fast growth of the video game industry, Zizzle's creative team remains in the hunt for new ideas that connect with kids, securing products linked with *High School Musical* on the Disney Channel, which includes a karaoke microphone, and an interactive dance mat.

At 54 years old, now regarded as an experienced legend in the industry, Roger Shiffman remains innovative, while continuing to uncover the competitive edge in toy making. Even as the toy industry slipped into a slight decline in the past few years in overall revenue, Shiffman's new start-up of Zizzle is just getting started, with plans of execution and more exciting toy industry victories on the way.

Like Shiffman's example at Tiger Electronics and Zizzle, a competitive effort must be a part of a company's successful equation. Each form of *art* will have its own criteria of value and its own modes of execution. In every competitive *art* form you will find yourself faced with a natural hierarchy. People tend to pay more for the *art* that they value more, and pay less, if anything, for the *art* that they value less.

As a young man raised within the crowded and competitive neighborhood of West Philadelphia, I originally chose to focus on football over basketball, which was equally popular, because I was a better performer at it. I was not particularly tall, and I did not play basketball enough to acquire the necessary skills to continue to play at a competitive level. With more focus on football, I was able to improve in the sport.

But as a college student, when football became increasingly competitive, I had another choice to make. I could either push myself with *love* to compete at the next level, and possibly fail or become mediocre, or refocus on a goal that would better suit my professional strengths.

With solid math and science grades to compete, the field of pharmacy was not a bad choice for me. Nevertheless, I found that by moving into the field of English, and finally Print Journalism, I was able to become even more competitive in my craft by selecting a stronger *art* to *love*.

In opposition to loving what you do as the initiator of success, sometimes your particular *art* may not start with *love* at all. My *art* became writing and communication, not because I loved it or wanted to do it initially, but because I found that I was good at it. And when curious people have asked me what inspired me to become a writer, I have been consistent with the truth; "I was good at it." Writing allowed me to compete at the top of the *pyramid*, where football and pharmacy did not.

Fortunately, I was adept enough to make a career transition early and move into the profession that better suited me. Other individuals may take years to make the same assessment and move themselves into a field of work where they are better suited to compete. But it is never too late to make a necessary change.

However, one thing concerning the production and competition of *art* is certain. No one can sell what he doesn't possess. If you do not create any *art* or represent any art form that has been created or will be performed, then you will not be compensated for any artistic services. And if everything that we create is *art*, then what is any man or woman worth without a valuable art form to become passionate about, to utilize, to support or to invest in?

A secretary types, organizes the office, directs phone calls, and makes sure the day runs smoothly for the busy managers and executives. A caterer prepares food that appeals to the senses and feeds our hunger. A cable guy determines the problem with your cable wiring and fixes the reception on the television. An auto mechanic performs diagnostic tests on the various systems of a car and gets it running again. Then you pay these professionals for their artistic services accordingly.

So what is your *art*? What skills or services do you perform or provide that are good enough to place a value on? And if you don't have any, then you need to seriously think about acquiring some. Otherwise, you'll be forced to take whatever job or occupation that life has left to offer you.

CHAPTER 11

WHY THE COLOR GOLD?

Gold is the name and descriptive color of the precious metallic element that has been valued by human civilization for thousands of years. The malleable element of gold has been used to create coins, jewelry, and various artifacts of social wealth. Throughout history, gold has been a constant symbol of riches, illumination, and benevolence. The metallic glare of gold added to *art*, structures, or buildings has been inspirational. And gold creations have been treasured as the essence or finest exemplification of their kind.

There are few elements in nature that radiate as brightly as gold. When the rays of sunlight strikes it, the result is blinding. Like the Egyptian pharaohs, who commissioned the greatest builders to raise the symbolic golden pyramids in their honor, kings, queens, chiefs, and lords have all produced boundless artifacts of gold to represent their influence and positions of leadership within society. These golden artifacts were all melted, shaped, and designed by creative, and inspired artists.

Greek civilization of the fourth and fifth centuries B.C., "the Golden Age," is deemed one of most dominant eras of artistic merit and enlightenment. However, historians have understood for centuries that the golden years of excellence in the West, were thousands of years late. African, Asian, East Indian, and Native American civilizations had discovered the inspirational qualities of *art* and the illumination of gold thousands of years ago.

Individuals who were deemed to have a golden glow were considered special, like the glow of Mexican-American boxer, former Olympian, six-time world champion, and successful entrepreneur, Oscar De La Hoya.

Coined the Golden Boy, and the only United States boxing team member to win a gold medal in the 1992 Olympics in Barcelona, Spain, it was immediately assumed that De La Hoya would rise to the highest rank in professional boxing in his weight class. Young, handsome, bilingual, and charming, Oscar had already won gold medals in the U.S. Olympic Cup, the Goodwill Games, the U.S. National Championships, the USA vs. Olympic Festival, the USA vs. Boxing National Championships, USA vs. Bulgaria, and a gold in the 1992 World Challenge.

In the field of professional boxing, a multibillion-dollar industry, De La Hoya was viewed as a can't-miss talent, and well worth the investment of his promoters and boxing fans. Born and raised in East Los Angeles, he had worked to perfect his considerable skills in the *art* of boxing from an early age, compiling an amateur record of 223–5 with 164 by knockout. As a professional with high expectations, he would not disappoint.

De La Hoya won his first 11 fights, 10 by knockout, and won his first boxing championship as a junior lightweight in only his 12th professional bout in March 1994, before his 21st birthday. He later moved up in weight class five times to defeat an unprecedented record of 12 world champions, while winning titles in six weight divisions, and generating nearly $600 million in cable pay-per-view buys alone.

Inside the ring, Oscar De La Hoya became the richest fighter of all time, compiling a professional record of 39 wins and 5 losses, with 30 by knockout. He was named *The Ring* magazine's Fighter of the Year in 1995, and was regarded as the best Pound for Pound fighter in the world in 1997.

Outside of the ring, as Oscar's phenomenal career in professional boxing began to wind down, he produced several successful boxing shows with HBO, designed a clothing line, released a Grammy-nominated CD—with songs in both English and Spanish—starred in and hosted a boxing reality television series on the Fox network, established his own boxing promotions company, Golden Boy Promotions, and acquired several sports-based magazines, including *The Ring, KO, World Boxing*, and *Pro Wrestling Illustrated*, all owned by Golden Boy Enterprises.

Proving himself to be as competitive in the gold *art* of business as he has been in the ring, De La Hoya's Golden Boy Promotions recently formed a partnership with Anschutz Entertainment Group (AEG), a world leader in live sports and entertainment, to push his promotions brand to #1 in the boxing industry, with nearly 50 boxers under contract. The deal included acquisition of ownership shares of the AEG-owned Houston Dynamos in major league soccer, of which Oscar had shown an interest.

Regarding his partnership with AEG, Oscar "Golden Boy" De La Hoya stated, "They have proven themselves over the years to be the best of the best, and we look forward to a long and productive relationship with them."

Like Oscar's ascension to the boxing throne from East LA, the color gold is meant to shine with ambition, and to rise up from dust like a symbolic *pyramid*. So if you are afraid to stand and deliver, afraid to compete, afraid to be judged, afraid to lead, and afraid to be your best, then gold is not the color for you. Gold is for people who possess enough talent, ingenuity, and confidence to stand before their *art* and be held accountable for it. Always!

Gold is what is meant by *adoration, presentation, purpose, execution,* and *excellence*. These are The Five Elements of art. Art is adorable. And *adoration* is best represented by the color gold.

CHAPTER 12

ADORATION

The definition of *adoration* in *Webster's Third New International Dictionary* is the act or state of adoring or being adored, or regarding with admiration. It is also the object or recipient of the act of adoring.

Adoration is reserved for those who are deemed qualified to receive praise. Well, praise is not easily given to underachievers, nor is it typically given to the masses. Conversely, it is the usually the masses who give high praise to the one. The farther you descend from the position of first—as in second, third, fourth, fifth, or sixth—the less *adoration* you can expect to receive from the public.

Therefore, we may argue that, in order to be adored, one must strive toward a full mastery of personal, team, or company skills. This is what we mean when we say that someone is good at what he does. We can all tell ourselves that we are better than average or sufficient in our individual skills; but it is the masses of public opinion, or the assessments of the knowledgeable few, who ultimately determine the recognition of those who indeed stand out.

Adoration is the first indicator of marketable *art*, or artistic gifts. When one recognizes the golden glow of talent within an individual, or the exceptional value of a creative product, the validation of that person or object can quickly lead to a craving for more. Talented people and valuable products then build more acclaim, and their praise becomes the added fuel for a lifelong journey of achievements, support, and community and business stature.

Such a product was formed in 1886 when pharmacist John Stith Pemberton created the formula for Coca-Cola, producing a syrup-based, nonalcoholic, high-carbohydrate drink that would take the public by storm and maintain its *adoration* for more than a hundred years. The formula and brand was bought by Asa Candler in 1889, who incorporated the Coca-Cola Company in 1892.

Coca-Cola is now recognized as the #1 soft drink and beverage brand in the world, with products sold in more than 300 countries. But although the Coca-Cola Company offers a huge number of new soft drinks and beverage products, including Fanta, Sprite, Minute Maid Juices, Powerade, Nestea, Fruitopia fruit drink, Dasani water, and the recently purchased Glacéau flavored vitamin water, the original Coca-Cola (Classic) remains adored by millions globally.

Like the Coca-Cola brand soft drink, an individual or company becomes adored in business as the source of public reverence and inspiration. Film director Steven Spielberg became an inspiration early on in his career through a masterful direction of a 1975 summer beach horror movie entitled *Jaws*. The film—based on a Peter Benchley novel about a man-eating shark who wreaks havoc on a small beach town—became an instant classic, grossing more than $470 million at the box office, and broke all previous film records, spawning what is now referred to as the season of "summer blockbusters," between the months of May through July.

At the age of 29, Spielberg, the upstart filmmaker, who had failed on three separate applications to attend the highly regarded film school at the University of Southern California because of low grades, became one of America's youngest multimillionaires, and was given a great deal of creative control over his future film projects. Proving that his talent was not a fluke, Spielberg, who attended California State University at Long Beach, went on to write and direct his next feature film, a science-fiction project entitled *Close Encounters of the Third Kind* in 1977, which became another box office and critically acclaimed hit.

Spielberg would increase his *adoration* as a gifted filmmaker by teaming up with *Star Wars* creator and friend George Lucas, to direct the adventure film, *Raiders of the Lost Ark* in 1981, the first of four successful Indiana Jones movies. *Raiders of the Lost Ark* became the biggest hit of the year and is still considered a landmark example of an action film. It was nominated for various film awards, which had become the norm for Steven Spielberg films.

He then returned to the science fiction genre a year later, to direct *E.T. the Extra-Terrestrial*, the story of a young boy and a lost-and-found alien that the boy befriends. Topping Spielberg's record again, *E.T.* became the highest grossing film of all time until Spielberg bested his record a third time with the direction of *Jurassic Park* in 1993, based on a Michael Crichton novel.

For nearly four decades, Steven Spielberg has proven himself again and again as one of the most innovative and adored filmmakers in history, while writing, directing, or producing more than 30 feature films—a number of which he has been nominated for best picture or best director honors—including *The Color Purple*, *Schindler's List*, *Saving Private Ryan*, *Munich*, and *Letters from Iwo Jima*.

Understanding his *adoration* within the film industry, with films grossing nearly $8 billion internationally, Spielberg formed an independent studio partnership with business friends, David Geffen and Jeffrey Katzenberg, to create DreamWorks in the mid 1990s. Spielberg is now estimated to have built a personal fortune of $3 billion, and has influenced the popularity of big event movies more than any other filmmaker. Covering multiple genres, subjects, and family themes within his films, Spielberg continues to create, direct, and produce successful feature projects, including another summer blockbuster, his recent *Indiana Jones and the Kingdom of the Crystal Skull*, where he collaborated again with George Lucas.

Although many of you are unable to imagine yourselves as successful or as adored as the Coca-Cola brand soft drink, or the Steven Spielberg library of films, sometimes the *adoration* of others can open up a particular industry for our own dreams and aspirations to follow. Such was the case with my career as an author.

Had it not been for the breakout success of Terry McMillan, a fellow journalism major out of the University of California at Berkeley, who self-promoted her first two contemporary novels before striking gold with her third title, *Waiting to Exhale* in 1992, I have no idea whether my books would have ever caught on with an urban readership. McMillan's brand of frank dialogue and realistic relationships spawned a new following and a national interest in contemporary African-American literature.

After graduating from Berkeley, McMillan moved east to New York to study film at Columbia University, earning a master's degree in the early 1980s. She later enrolled in a writing workshop at the Harlem Writer's Guild, where she would begin to pen her first novel, *Mama*, published in 1987. Becoming a single mother with a hard life of addictions in New York, McMillan relocated for a fresh start and a job as an associate professor at the University of Arizona in 1988.

While in Arizona, McMillan wrote her second novel *Disappearing Acts*, published in 1989, which won more praise and critical acclaim than her first book. By the time she had done the groundwork for her third novel, by sending out thousands of letters to libraries and organizations to promote her books, while performing readings at every book store that would have her, Terry McMillan's *Waiting to Exhale* took the publishing industry totally by surprise.

The contemporary novel of four professional African-American women, who struggle to balance their careers and personal relationships, catapulted to #1 on the *New York Times* bestseller's list for fiction, and remained at the top of the list for months, while selling four million copies. The book was soon as highly regarded as Alice Walker's *The Color Purple*, which Steven Spielberg had directed as a successful film adaptation nearly a decade earlier in the 1980s, starring Whoopi Goldberg and Oprah Winfrey. Likewise, *Waiting to Exhale* became an adored film production, staring award-winning singer Whitney Houston, and celebrated actress Angela Bassett.

With the overwhelming success of McMillan's contemporary tale, major publishing houses became eager to offer lucrative contracts to upcoming African-American writers, including me at age 26. And when Terry McMillan published her fourth novel, *How Stella Got Her Groove Back* in 1996, her initial print run had increased from a few thousand in softback for her first book in 1987, to 800,000 in hard back for her fourth book—a new record for a first print of an African-American title.

Despite the previous apprehension of the publishing industry concerning a largely untapped African-American audience of readers, McMillan claimed that black Americans would indeed read books that related to their experiences, and the publishing industry was forced to believe her. McMillan quickly became an adored and recognizable spokeswoman in the publishing industry across race, gender, and class lines, inspiring an Oprah Winfrey book club that spawned women's reading groups across America, while increasing print runs, marketing and sales, and publishing opportunities for many African-American novelists, including increased attention for celebrated mystery writer Walter Mosley, science fiction writer Octavia Butler, and Pulitzer Prize and Nobel Prize–winning author Toni Morrison.

Since Terry's reign in the 1990s, when she became a multimillionaire novelist, as well an inspirational force within the publishing industry in less than a decade, the African-American literary genre has increased to more than $300 million annually in market revenue, with dozens of new writers and hundreds of different titles hitting book store and library shelves each year.

When it comes to *adoration*, companies would love to be able to predict which talented individuals or products will become The One that the public will adore. But since they can't, public praise continues to prove its human and corporate value. The next big thing is liable to come from any source. And when one is able to capture the *passion* of the masses, it eventually leads to great success and wealth.

Are you or your company innovative enough to produce products, goods, or services that may spark the next big wave of enterprise? Are you ready to take full advantage of new opportunities that may become available within your industry? How serious are you about mastering the competitive goals of your *art*?

The bottom line of *adoration* is this: families, friends, companies, and surrounding communities value people who have extraordinary skills, services, or products. Anyone can be average; but it takes the above average effort to become adored. So consider the following five ranking groups, and on a scale from 1 to 50 how would you honestly rank the recognition, worship, reverence, or honor that you or your company receives from those around you in regards to your skills, services, or products of *art*?

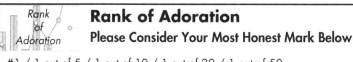

Rank of Adoration
Please Consider Your Most Honest Mark Below

#1 / 1 out of 5 / 1 out of 10 / 1 out of 20 / 1 out of 50

The key here is to define yourself as a specialist for a particular group. If you have chosen a highly popular *art* form or profession, your rank could easily be a number much greater than one; in which case, you become less valuable.

The ultimate goal of business is to find creative ways to expand the audience from the smallest unit to affect the largest community—where the individual is able to maintain uniqueness—while attracting greater interests. In other words, learn to be the best at what you do in your specific class, and stand out for it, so that you can eventually become adored—or at least, respected—by everyone.

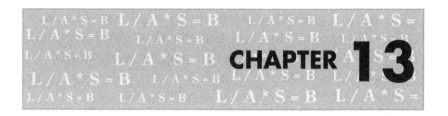

CHAPTER 13

PRESENTATION

Webster's Third New International Dictionary defines *presentation* as the act of presenting with the power and/or the privilege to bring into the presence of a group, particularly to introduce in a formal setting, as to a superior or a candidate.

No matter what business you are in, a *presentation* occurs in every single hour, on every single day, of every single week. They happen in a thousand corporate boardrooms, over office desks, over the Internet, conference telephone calls, inside elevators, lunchrooms, and over breakfast, lunch, and dinner.

In a *presentation*, you can expect to see charts, graphs, samples, drawings, pages of research, projections, past history, information sources, mission statements, Power Point equipment, projector machines, dark rooms, auditoriums—even, at times, live performances.

The *presentation* is where you display the functions, meaning, and value of your *art;* either for selling, for investment, for honor, or for corporate votes and backing within the larger company. And as with all other elements of *art* that we'll discuss in this Gold Section, a *presentation* should be compelling if one expects to garner a positive response or gain from it. On the other hand, a bad *presentation*, or none at all, can often equal the loss of an opportunity.

A successful *presentation* requires preparation, organization, confidence, visual materials, strong communication, and often a good business suit if it's being delivered within the corporate arena. But more than anything, a successful *presentation* takes audacity, an iron will to believe in what you're presenting.

In the post-apartheid nation of South Africa, Patrice Motsepe, a young and ambitious lawyer, had unquestionable faith in his entrepreneurial goal to acquire South African gold mines at a time in which the industry was beginning to decline. In the mid to late 1990s, the price of South African gold was dropping, forcing many of its profitable mining companies to sell or shut down their older, low-producing mine shafts.

Through an intense study of his nation's most lucrative industry, while representing mining companies, Motsepe kept a sharp eye on what made some mines succeed and others fail. Realizing that leaner companies were more successful, with less corporate overhead, Motsepe made his first move by starting a small labor company with contracts to sweep the low-level mines. By 1997, he was ready to own mine shafts of his own.

Motsepe's *presentation* to South African banks and investors was that he could run a better and more profitable mine shaft through use of a smaller work force, leaner management, and more strategic work shifts. Believing Motsepe to be a mad man who would embarrass black South Africans through a major business failure, the banks and established mining companies refused to back him. His plans were viewed as delirious. What made a lawyer-turned-businessman believe that he could run a better mine than the massive companies who had decades of experience?

To the rescue was Bobby M. Godsell, who was then a chief executive of the gold and uranium division at Anglo, a leading South African mining company. Godsell, who had worked to bring South African business leaders together with African National Congress officials at the end of apartheid, desired to help black South Africans get into business. He wanted to create new businessmen out of people who essentially had no start-up capital. Motsepe fit the bill.

In a move that would make South African history, Godsell believed enough in Motsepe's ideas of lean business, that he turned over Anglo's low-producing mine shafts to the lawyer/ entrepreneur for an $8.2 million payment plan, with a percentage of future profits. Forming his new mining company, called ARMgold, Motsepe would implement his tighter operations style of management, and pay off the $8.2 million debt within three years.

Motsepe would later invest in a cooperative deal with Anglo Platinum, the world's largest producer, to develop the new platinum mine of Modikwa. One after another, Motsepe's lean operating style would align him with more lucrative deals for his company. And as the price of gold began to rise, in 2002, Motsepe's ARMgold was strong enough to become listed on the Johannesburg Stock Exchange.

As Motsepe's company continued to grow and diversify into mines of nickel, chrome, iron, manganese and coal, ARMgold swallowed up partnerships with several old mining companies, and merge with Harmony, a gold mining company, and Avmin, a miner of base and precious metals, with divisions in Zambia, Congo, and Namibia. Motsepe's steadily rising company would soon become known as simply ARM.

Continuing in his ambitions, Motsepe pledged in 2005 that ARM would double in its size by 2010. The following year, the company struck a $360 million coal deal with Xstrata Plc, and took a minority stake in the Swiss-headquartered coal mining company's operations in South Africa.

Now at age 46, Patrice Motsepe's personal wealth has risen to an estimated $2.4 billion, making him South Africa's first black billionaire, while joining the list of top ten mining fortunes in the world. And it all started with his belief in an outlandish *presentation* to the South African establishment that he could run a leaner gold-mining operation.

Although not as profitable or expansive as Motsepe's fortune, I have been successful in quite a few presentations of my own, including a marketing *presentation* in 1999 that led to my ascension on the *New York Times* bestseller's list in 2000, a new contract *presentation* in 2000 that led to an undisclosed, major-figure publishing deal in 2001, and a business book *presentation* in 2007 that landed this opportunity to publish my first nonfiction title in 2009.

I presented *The Equation* to several members of the editorial staff at the John Wiley & Sons offices, signaling a major transition in my career from a creative writer of fiction to a knowledge-based writer of nonfiction. I ran through my group of Red, Gold, Green, and Purple cue cards, explaining the meaning of *The Equation*, how it works, all 4 of its components, its 20 elements, and how I planned to push it on a lecture series; not only throughout the United States, but internationally. I explained that *The Equation* was not only analytical, but universally mathematical. And I had been lecturing about the components of *The Equation* for 10 years.

As an eager journalist/entrepreneur, much like Motsepe, I have been very much at ease with the idea of presenting my observations, research, services, and artistic products as a part of creative and business competition. A personal *presentation* allows a company or group to understand your unique and passionate attachment to your ideas. Other artists would rather allow their agents, managers, or lawyers to introduce and close the business agreements for them. But I actually like the intense, face-to-face questions, answers, and eventual handshakes of the deal. Sometimes, you may be the only person who can explain it all successfully. And although preparing and delivering a winning *presentation* is not everyone's strength, it is indeed a vital element of business that all professionals and companies need to become familiar with.

Another definition of *presentation* is the act of setting forth for the notice of an audience, and or with a display, exhibition or show, including pictorial, theatrical displays, or symbols.

This meaning of the word brings to mind the example of the legendary Barnum & Bailey Circus. Partnered by the competitors James Anthony Bailey and P.T. Barnum in 1881, the Barnum & Bailey partnership would lead the world in circus acts, presented to the public for nearly a century as "The Greatest Show on Earth." Their phenomenal and exaggerated presentations would continue to draw attention worldwide.

"The Barnum & Bailey Circus presents Jumbo, the largest elephant in the world! Gather around, folks, and see an amazing sight that you've never seen before! The most ferocious tigers straight from the jungles of Siberia!"

Not only did they have outlandish circus announcements, but intriguing posters to match. Posters of Barnum & Bailey Circus acts with striking print, bright colors, and crowded artwork would promote it all, from the rare acts to the bizarre attractions.

With Barnum and Bailey both passing on, in 1907 their circus partnership was acquired by the Ringling Brothers, a family show of acrobats from the Midwest, who traveled with their own circus. Combining both shows as the Ringling Bros. and Barnum & Bailey Circus in the 1920s, John Ringling, the remaining owner, would become one of the richest men in the world before the decline of business in the Great Depression of the 1930s.

The circus promoters were geniuses at presenting ideas that would mesmerize the human mind, leading to all forms of promotional copycats. Long before the invention of television and feature films, both Barnum and Bailey realized that people would gladly pay to see performances that were over-the-top and unusual. If the promoters could not count on the acrobatic feats of the Ringling Brothers alone to bring out a crowd, then they would add a 400-pound muscle man to lift 10 midgets on a pole—or any show that would excite an audience.

The Barnum & Bailey philosophy was simple: if you want people to pay attention and come one, come all, then you can never afford to toss your product onto the public market without the necessary buildup or hype. The Barnum & Bailey circus had used the same principle that countless others have used since then: if you desire a heightened result, then learn how to present your *art*, services, or performance to a crowd with something extra. You must always remember to convince an audience that what you have to offer is worth their time, their money, and their full attention.

A *presentation* is also used to honor people or organizations for their great achievements. At many promoted ballroom affairs around the world, high-ranking individuals and companies have received awards for their excellence in various selected fields. I have been awarded many plaques, trophies, figurines, and framed certificates on numerous occasions myself, highlighted by a 2001 NAACP Image Award (National Association for the Advancement of Colored People) for "Outstanding Work of Literature in Fiction." I had no idea I would even be nominated that year, let alone win the award. Nevertheless, I had worked hard and purposefully to hone my *art* as a writer to earn the prestigious honor.

Although we may not all become as fortunate as Patrice Motsepe in our individual presentations, be able to reproduce the hype of a Barnum & Bailey circus, or receive a nationally recognized award for our efforts, as I noted at the beginning of this chapter, there are daily presentations that are performed by competitive and confident people all around the world. There are also various forms of recognition that are presented to standout professionals, companies, and employees, right on down to the title of The Employee of the Week.

So the question this chapter poses is this: are you one of the competitive people or companies, who perform in their profession well enough to present a new product, goal, or service to the corporation or to the general community—as well as receive an award, an advance, or any form of recognized *presentation* to celebrate your personal or company achievements? And if so, how would you rank the specialty of that *presentation* in your particular field?

Rank of Presentation
Please Consider Your Most Honest Mark Below

#1 / 1 out of 5 / 1 out of 10 / 1 out of 20 / 1 out of 50

We will uncover all of the details of your rankings in the final section, "The Equation in Use." However, if you are indeed an Employee of the Week or of the Month at your particular company, please understand that thousands of other companies present this same award 12 to 50 times a year. We therefore cannot regard that *presentation* as anything more than 1 out of 50 in its rank. However, if you are awarded the Employee of the Year at a Top 10 company, you may be allowed to move up in your ranking accordingly. The same formula holds true for those who are able to successfully present new products, services, or goals at top-rated companies or in front of big money investors.

For instance, if you were able to successfully present a product, service, or company goal at the offices of Google or Microsoft—two companies that are currently engaged in battle for the #1 position in computer technology—then you could very well rank in the top 1 out of 5 in your field, with no argument. Even if you were unsuccessful, you could argue for 1 out of 10, or 1 out of 20, simply by virtue of being able to place yourself in that high-stakes room.

Remember that Microsoft's billionaire cofounder Bill Gates, was once able to successfully present his goals, services, and products at the IBM offices in Florida—when *they* were the computer kings three decades ago. I would consider that a #1 *presentation*. And look at Mr. Bill Gates now.

We must also take into account—as I pointed out at the end of the chapter on *passion*—that our rankings will naturally change over time depending on where we are: the *beginning*, *peak*, or *decline* or our respective careers. So where a *presentation* to IBM was most highly regarded in 1980, after the explosion of advancements made in computer technology during the Silicon Valley era of the past three decades, a #1 rank for IBM cannot be substantiated in 2009. IBM has now been pushed back into a Top 5—or even Top 10—in computer technology, while fighting to remain in contention.

CHAPTER 14

PURPOSE

Webster's Third New International Dictionary defines *purpose* as something that one sets before oneself as an object to be attained; an end or an aim to be kept in view in any plan, measure, exertion or operation. In other words, *"What is the purpose, aim, or objective of your business? And what is the ultimate goal of your professional journey?"*

Many individuals would give the basic answer that they are attempting to earn a living. Well, of course. In an economic world of supply, demand, production, goods, and currency, we are all trying to make a living. But as your living applies to your specific *art*, the mastery of a certain profession becomes *more* than just making a living, the *purpose* of your particular *art* becomes your legacy. In other words, *"What will you become known for?"*

Since a huge part of our adult lives is based on the influences, events, and preparations of our youth, career *purpose* is many times embedded in our character from early on. For ages, psychologists have analyzed the effects of a person's childhood and how that childhood later affects her decisions and way of life as an adult. Accordingly, many of our business decisions are made as a result of the particular challenges, understandings, struggles, and victories of our upbringing.

John Davison Rockefeller, Sr., an American legend in the oil industry, became one of the wealthiest self-made businessmen in history as a direct result of the challenges of his upbringing. His determined *purpose* was to maximize his wealth and maintain it for the betterment of his family and of his nation.

Rockefeller became severely challenged in his youth by the instability and deceptive cunning of his father, William Avery Rockefeller, also known as "Big Bill" amongst a host of other erroneous names. A man of various schemes, Big Bill would collect whatever hustled wages he could muster through misleading the unsophisticated citizens in the towns that surrounded their home. It was even rumored that William had only married John D.'s mother, Eliza Davison, in a scheme to attain her father's land.

Due to his father's frequent and unexplained absences, the young Rockefeller—as the eldest son of the family—had no choice but to help his mother make due, tend to the land, pay their bills, and help provide for his younger siblings. When his family was later forced to move with Big Bill to the Midwest—after a deterioration of opportunities in the Northeast—John D. would experience even more volatility, with his father leaving the family to fend for themselves at the crowded Midwest homes of friends and relatives.

As Rockefeller continued to cope with his family's quicksand lifestyle, and remained the responsible young man of the house, his father continued to scramble around the countryside, scheming for inadequate profits. William Rockefeller's instability—particularly his penchant of giving and taking family money based on his own personal needs, while they struggled with want—left John D. obsessed to secure his family's income by any means necessary. He also vowed to reform his personal and business habits with a determined *purpose* to maintain stability, in opposition to his father's unpredictability.

By the time Rockefeller was able to land solid employment of his own, as a teenaged bookkeeper at a merchant and shipping company in Cleveland, he was virtual a man-child of experience and fortitude. Once gainfully employed, he declared that he would work his hardest to make sure that his family would never have to live through economic insecurities again. He wanted to ensure not only his personal wealth, but wealth in *excess* in order to safeguard his family's future. It was the only way for him to abolish the panic that his father had forced upon them.

As he matured into an assertive and capable businessman, John D. Rockefeller would build, protect, invest, and master a consistent method to achieve prosperity through which he and his family would never have to worry about chasing a dollar or going without. The experiences of his upbringing had prepared him to become a shrewd and strategic master in the *art* of contracts and negotiations. And in his later years—after establishing himself in the industry of oil and refineries—Rockefeller used what he had been forced to learn in his youth, and conceived tireless plans to increase the size and stability of his wealth. Not one dime was taken for granted or lost in the shuffle.

However, in the 1870s, the oil business proved to be as volatile as Rockefeller's father had been with his family's income. Each time a new oil well was discovered on an unexpected property, a new competitor became free to market his new oil at lower prices, sending the established oilmen scrambling to lower their own prices to remain in business. Such an unstable market forced wealthy oilmen into a constant state of panic, an economic nightmare that Rockefeller knew all too well. He viewed this irregular pricing as a major hindrance to business, while planning ways to secure an upper hand in the industry.

In the meantime, Rockefeller decided to invest more money and attention to oil refining, which led to the establishment of the Standard Works refineries. Akin to Bill Gates' masterful prediction of computer software in the twentieth century, John D. foresaw that the refining of oil into usable forms would eventually be more important than finding the wells. Just as computers would need software in order to run, oil would need to be refined in order to be used—no matter *who* found it.

Rockefeller was then committed by faith to become the one man capable of stabilizing the situation. He felt, with intense religious zeal, that amassing and controlling wealth was his life's mission. A fervent churchgoer who rejected alcohol, smoking, lavish showmanship, and all the other lewd and boisterous behavior that his father embraced, John deemed that God alone had set in motion the elements of his life, so that he would be prepared to lead his nation's most lucrative industry for the betterment of all.

Rockefeller's unrivaled drive to outwit the naysayers—who were not ingenious enough to find a workable solution to their common problems with oil—only made him more determined to organize his plans for consolidation. With superior strategy and *purpose*, the Standard Oil Company, a joint-stock firm with John D. Rockefeller as president—was born.

In the years that followed, Rockefeller's unwavering ideas and dogged faith would eventually win over his dissenters, and allow him to gobble up competitive refineries, strategic real estate, complementary industries, lucrative railroad agreements, and one oil partnership after another—until he would controlled the majority of the oil wells, refineries, and oil company stock in America.

Despite an historic vilification that John D. Rockefeller would acquire as the mastermind of American trusts, cartels, and unfair business practices—which led a number of governmental agencies to fight against such obvious consolidation of wealth and industry in the future—Rockefeller's self-righteous idea to become wealthy under God for the betterment of all, eventually proved valid. The Rockefeller family and the Rockefeller Foundation would later become one of the most active, capable, and capitalized organizations of charity in the arts, sciences, medicine, education, race relations, architecture, and general advancement of the national community.

Rockefeller once decreed that a progressive man must sometimes go against the grain to meet his goals. And he proved this by becoming one of the most important figures in American business history, in spite of an infamous reputation. Now more than five generations later, the Rockefeller family fortune and legacy remains intact.

Like John D. Rockefeller's unmatched example, the *purpose* of your career serves to reinforce your diligence. *Purpose* is the element of business that will make the drive to attain your goals much stronger. To become the best, and competitive within your field, your *purpose* must be *more* than just to make a living. Your *purpose* must be to *succeed* and to *excel* in your mission. Otherwise, you will find yourself out of contention, joining those who live and work without *purpose*, and who generally allow all forms of hurdles and setbacks to impede their progress.

But individuals and groups who move forward have a *purpose*. As the saying goes, "What won't kill you, will only make you stronger." So if you presently have no particular *purpose* for your business, it will be very beneficial to develop one that will sufficiently motivate you to succeed beyond all difficulties. Because difficulties will arise.

Where the *purpose* of amassing and stabilizing excess wealth— to secure and safeguard his family and nation—was the goal of John D. Rockefeller Sr., as a young, entrepreneurial writer, my *purpose* was to create contemporary literature of African-American culture. My goal was not only to make a living, but to inspire readership, intelligent comprehension, empathy, and dialogue concerning the importance of numerous human perspectives.

Every nation of people has stories that need to be told and that need to connect to the universe of humanity. So once I realized that I had become more than adequate at writing the stories of my nation within a nation, it became my mission, not only to continue to write and to publish, but to *improve* my writing skills each year by taking on the new challenge of presenting original and thought-provoking material.

That specific mission—to challenge myself and others to continue in our thirst for knowledge and understanding—was what drove me to write 16 novels in 16 consecutive years on 16 different subjects, regardless of how they all sold on the marketplace. Had my goal been only to make a living, or to write a popular story that sells, then maybe I would have only written nine books on three subjects, while stressing all of my gains and losses.

However, within any competitive industry, the *purpose* of leadership is often to create new paths, where there may be no precedent. Sometimes these new paths create new wealth, sometimes they don't. Nevertheless, my *purpose* has remained consistent, and so has the advancement of my *art*. But as a progressive entrepreneur, the need to diversify in order to stimulate and maintain economic growth is a necessity of business.

Therefore, my *purpose* now transitions to utilizing my *art* to affect more people by uncovering the universal components of successful business. These components and elements are valuable assets that I have learned to understand in my experiences—as well as those I have observed through others. I am now sharing these with you.

As my now *art* expands to incorporate a larger audience, my *purpose*, aim, and mission remains the same—to challenge us *all* to continue to learn. And my drive to continue to write and to explore the challenges of human intelligence, progress, and business remains as strong as it ever was—and even stronger.

That is the meaning and power of *purpose*. Faith in a *purpose* all by itself, is enough to keep a person on course for many years. So for those of you who still do not have one, it is time for us to be honest with ourselves again. What is the *purpose* that you have set for yourself, or your goal in your career or company? And how would you rank your aim to keep that *purpose* in view as compared to those around you?

Rank of Purpose
Please Consider Your Most Honest Mark Below

#1 / 1 out of 5 / 1 out of 10 / 1 out of 20 / 1 out of 50

Without a doubt, I would consider a rank of *purpose* to be the hardest thing for many of us to assess. Some of the people who claim to have the highest *purpose* will inevitably be the least successful. That is the competitive nature of a true artist—and it makes sense; the higher the *purpose*, the harder the work. Nevertheless, the higher the achievement, the longer the legacy.

CHAPTER 15

EXECUTION

Webster's Third New International Dictionary defines *execution* as the act or process of executing; performance or accomplishment. This definition hits the nail on the head. *Execution* is the act, mode, or result of performance in any of the arts, or in anything that requires a special skill or technique.

That's what this Gold Section is all about: *execution.* Can you execute well enough to be considered a valuable artist in your field of work? Every occupation requires that you excel in a particular skill or technique—even jobs that are considered easy or run of the mill. If a client or customer is expected to consistently spend a competitive dollar for a particular product or service, then that company had better be *good* at what they do. Otherwise, another qualified, harder working, and more innovative company may steal away the business. That's the basic concept of the free market. We have the freedom to trade with whomever we believe to be the best individual or company to serve our interests.

Either you get the job done, or you don't. However, when it comes to prospective business, the act of pitching a sell is all about having the confidence or track record to tell a potential customer that you can indeed execute the job—and doing so well before you actually perform it. Such *execution* with confidence brings to mind the lifetime investing career of Warren Buffett, chairman and CEO of Berkshire Hathaway.

They call him the "Oracle of Omaha," with a net worth of more than $60 billion. A precocious kid, born in Omaha, Nebraska, Buffett bought his first company stock at age 11. He filed his first tax return at 13. And before he ever graduated from college at the University of Nebraska in 1949, he was well on his way to mastering the *art* of studying investments, and the rising and falling values of companies. To help solidify his methods, Buffett went on to study under the investment guru Benjamin Graham at Columbia University—where he earned a master's degree in economics in 1951.

Graham—referred to as the "father of value investing"—believed that every company was bound to trade at prices below its value sooner or later. And any investor could become wealthy by thoroughly studying companies and investing in their stock at their low points. Buffett learned his lessons well, invested in Berkshire Hathaway—a struggling textile company—in the early 1960s and took control by 1965. He then continued buying undervalued companies, while investing in the sure-fire stocks of Coca-Cola, Procter & Gamble, American Express, Gillette, and other brand-name companies that continued to dominate their particular markets.

But before you become intimidated by Buffett's present-day status and income—and consider his case out of reach to learn from—one only needs to study his simple principles of investing to apply his methods of successful *execution* to your own life.

Buffett has advised investors to invest only in companies that they know and understand. Well, you would be hard pressed to find many adults in American who have never heard of Coca-Cola. Coca-Cola is practically everywhere. That's a no-brainer investment. You buy it and you drink it.

Buffett has advised investors to buy when people are fearful and sell when people are greedy. Well, if we know anything about economic security, people tend sell themselves short and accept whatever they can get when they are unfortunately involved in a crisis. On the other hand, wealthy individuals have shown tendencies to overpay for products and services, particularly when they begin to feel invincible. So catch a rattled man to buy from, and an eager rich man to sell to.

Buffett has also advised investors to buy companies and not stocks. Well, without the bankroll or access to capital, it's a little hard for the average person to buy a company. Nevertheless, let's understand the logic behind the advice. If a department store has a going-out-of-business sale, where everything must go, are you going to buy more items or less? The no-brainer is to buy *more*. Most likely, every item in the store will be sold at less than *half* its retail value. And if you had a few thousand dollars, and happen to be a real entrepreneur, you could buy enough items to create your own neighborhood flee market, advertised through basic print fliers. You then sell the clothing individually and make a cash profit off of every item.

Now how hard is that *execution* to understand? By buying undervalued companies, selling off their assets—while customarily leaving management teams in place—and flipping the profits into bigger and better acquisitions, Warren Buffett was able to grow his company rapidly. And those are just a few of the basic principles that allowed his company, Berkshire Hathaway, to become a consistent winner, while making its shareholders hundreds of millions of dollars in over 40 years of investing.

Once an individual or company has earned enough hard cash to go on an investment shopping spree, Buffett advises to wait for a good deal and always remember to make money by not losing money. That means you continue to do your homework and not become hasty and wasteful with your capital. In Berkshire's 40-year history, Buffett has only lost company value once in 2001, an amazing track record of success.

With investments in the *Washington Post*, and Geico Car Insurance—among the company's other holdings—by 1983, Buffett became one of the top earners on the *Forbes* list, with a net worth of $620 million. Berkshire then hit the New York Stock Exchange, creating the highest-priced stock at a whopping $4,300 a share. By the end of the decade in 1989, Buffett's net worth had increased to nearly $4 billion. As his company continued to increase its market value, Buffett was ranked as the richest American before being supplanted by Microsoft's Bill Gates in 1994.

Like many other strong businessmen, Buffett has been known to look to the future in determining which companies he can count on for prolonged success. When he could not determine which new technology companies were built to last during the rush to invest in the dot-com industry of the late 1990s, his Berkshire Hathaway became one of the few investment companies to avoid tremendous and embarrassing losses.

In the *art* of investments, Warren Buffett has proven to be second to none. However, the self-made billionaire has merely maintained his methods of *execution* to make it all happen. He continues to live in the same house he bought for under $32,000 in 1958, and speaks about his principles in plain, everyday language. In the present state of the American economy in a new presidential election year, he has now begun to take on a more public imagery than he's bothered with in the past, while dishing out advice more readily to any and all who are willing to listen to him.

Buffett has now begun to spread his investment search for undervalued companies abroad: in Europe, Asia, the Mediterranean, and the Middle East.

But what are your modes of *execution?* How do you plan to move ahead, compete, and get the job done in your particular field? As an expert investor, Mr. Buffett is not outside of the general laws of society, he simply planned his work and worked his plan, as we are *all* challenged to do.

Have you shown *execution* in your career: the act, mode, or result of performance of an *art* form that requires a special skill or technique? How would you rank your personal or company *execution* in your particular field as compared to those around you? Let's continue to be honest.

Rank of Execution

Please Consider Your Most Honest Mark Below

#1 / 1 out of 5 / 1 out of 10 / 1 out of 20 / 1 out of 50

Although versatility and the challenge of a greater goal may not be necessary to exact *execution*, variety is indeed a plus. However, if you are able to become the best at one small thing, instead of attempting many great things, then do so.

Refer to the final section, "The Equation in Use," for more details.

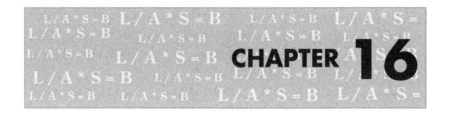

CHAPTER 16

EXCELLENCE

Webster's Third New International Dictionary defines *excellence* as the state of possessing good qualities in an eminent degree; an excellent or valuable quality. To further dissect its meaning, the root words of excellent—or to excel—are defined respectively as exceeding in high station or rank and to surpass or outshine. More concisely—*excellence* is to possess a distinguished *art* that shines like gold.

Among business leaders, the elements of *excellence*, team motivation, and drive have been reinforced through the books, speeches, and coaching disciples of American football legend, Vince Lombardi. In football, *excellence* is now traditionally awarded to the Super Bowl champion in the form of the Vince Lombardi Trophy, a glimmering replica of a golden football attached to an equally shiny, foot-high stand. The trophy was renamed for the legendary Green Bay Packers coach after his death in 1970.

Lombardi, born in Brooklyn, New York, in 1913, became revered in business circles as a proven winner and an admirable leader, who was consistent at motivating men to reach their full potential as individuals and as a team. The winner of five NFL Championships and the first two Super Bowl titles, in 1966 and

1967, Lombardi and the Packers became synonymous with team-work and corporate victory.

In his drive toward *excellence* in football, Lombardi attended Fordham University in the Bronx on a football scholarship. Undaunted by the larger players who competed around him, he played as an undersized offensive guard for a team that won 25 consecutive games and held many of their opponents scoreless. After receiving his bachelor's degree from Fordham in 1937, Vince floated from a position at a finance company, to a few stints of semi-pro football, and an incomplete attempt at a law degree from Fordham's night school, before he accepted a fateful assistant coaching position at St. Cecelia Catholic School in New Jersey at age 26.

Three years later, Lombardi held his first head coaching position at St. Cecelia's, before returning to Fordham to coach the university's freshman teams in football and basketball. After moving on to serve as offensive line coach at the U.S. Military Academy at West Point—under the leadership of coach Colonel Red Blaik—Lombardi would acquire the basis for his legendary coaching style of motivating grown, professional men.

Landing his first NFL job as an assistant with the New York Giants in 1954, Lombardi later accepted the position of head coach and general manager of the Green Bay Packers at age 45. He then created a brutal training and conditioning regimen for his team, expecting full *dedication* and effort from each player. In his first year as a professional football coach, Lombardi turned a group who had only won 2 out of 12 games the previous season into a 7-and-5 contender.

In his second year as head coach and general manager, Lombardi led his Packers to the 1960 NFL Championship game where they suffered a close loss that would solidify his philosophy of *excellence* for the championship years to come. In his book, *When Pride Still Mattered*, Lombardi declared that losing a championship game was unacceptable. He then inspired his teams to win all nine of their next playoff and championship games. And in nine seasons as a professional head coach, eight with Green Bay and one with the Washington Redskins in 1969, Lombardi would never endure a losing season, inspiring leaders in every walk of life to admire his leadership.

Considered a top-rank motivator, Lombardi became a frequent speaker, not only in the *art* of football, but in the methodologies of *excellence* in industry, while helping to establish the Green Bay Packers as one of the most storied, consistent, and profitable franchises in all of sports.

Featured as the face of the NFL on a *Time* magazine cover in December of 1962, Lombardi was enshrined in the Pro Football Hall of Fame in 1971 and later had grade schools, football fields, public parks, city streets, cancer centers, and clinics all named in his honor. With a proud statue standing outside of Green Bay's historical Lambeau Field, Lombardi's speeches on the winning formulas of desire, preparation, attitude, and *consistency* continue to be quoted by business leaders today.

Corporations have recognized Lombardi's ideas about discipline, *passion*, management, and consistent direction—the ideas that guided his players to become successful in their individual and team goals. Industry leaders understood that the goals of *excellence* in individual and team sports were the same goals that apply to individual and company business—to motivate individuals and groups to reach a high and consistent level of *execution*.

I was inspired by coaches to achieve *excellence* in my aspirations both as an athlete and as an individual. A member of the Oak Lane Youth Association in Philadelphia, I became a champion on three consecutive Police Athletic League (PAL) football teams from 1979 to 1981. In three straight seasons, I had no idea of what felt it like to lose, compiling an Oak Lane Wildcats record of 32 and 0, with an average win margin of more than 20 points a game, and plenty of shutout victories each year, including a 40-to-0 championship win over the Ivy Hill Saints in 1980. By the time I was 10, I had already learned how to practice hard, prepare to win, and expect *excellence*—principles I continued to follow for success in my adult life as an entrepreneur and a writer.

There is no substitute for acquired knowledge when it comes to *excellence*. We are all the living lessons that we have learned from others, or we learn on our own. Some of us have natural advantages that allow us more easily to attain resources that we need to succeed. Nevertheless, access to resources alone does not make us successful. The desire to execute at a higher-than-average level drives us all to develop the skills necessary to reach our goals—whether that success is in sports, academics, or business. The effective methods of success become addictive.

It was that same drive toward *excellence* that would inspire a young Ralph Lifschitz—who would become internationally known as Ralph Lauren—to acquire a $50,000 loan in 1967 to jump-start his brand of high-quality clothing. Born and raised in a middle-class family in the Bronx, the young Ralph had already begun to buy expensive clothing in his youth, so that he could stand out in style, even in grade school.

Lauren went on to study business at City College in Manhattan before dropping out. He then began to build his highly successful Polo brand in 1968, starting with a line of men's ties that catered to the professional men who wore Brooks Brothers suits.

After working at the tie manufacturer A. Rivetz & Company, Lauren began to design wide ties as the foundation of his Polo Fashions, instead of focusing on the slimmer model-sized tie. Bloomingdales advised him to shelve his brand name and remain faithful to the traditional-sized ties, if he wanted their stores to sell his products, but Lauren stuck to his guns and turned their restrictive offer down. He continued to build his name and create wide ties until popular demand won over, and forced the respected retailer to negotiate an agreement on Ralph Lauren's terms.

Building on the status and the image of Polo—a sport for the affluent—Ralph Lauren was able to establish not only a clothing line, but an image of an exquisite lifestyle. The name Polo was not chosen by accident; Lauren and his older brother had selected it by design, to signify *excellence* in clothing. And it worked.

Ralph Lauren and his Polo brand began to epitomize fashion. The brand added suits, women's clothing, home collections, western designs, fragrances, accessories, furniture, sports apparel, denim, exclusive labels, and a less expensive line of clothing for lower-end retailers.

To maintain the standard of *excellence* in his brand, Ralph Lauren has continued to stand by his quality, his high-end prices, his selection of style, his fashion leadership, and keen business sense to increase Polo's value to a nearly $4 billion a year company, with close to 300 stores in the United States and licenses to more than 100 manufacturers worldwide. And as hundreds of new clothing brands have come and gone, been sold to larger labels, and repackaged during Polo's 40 years in existence, Ralph Lauren has remained his company's CEO and chairman—controlling the majority of its voting power under the umbrella of the international L'Oréal company.

As the CEO of a major successful company, Lauren and other corporate-level artists have all risen from entrepreneurial pursuits to the top of the *art* pecking order within their respective fields. Like Vince Lombardi as the coach, the company CEO is there to guide the individual, staff and business as the most skilled, knowledgeable, and capable leader. And like Lombardi, Ralph Lauren has been that most skilled leader—who has inspired *adoration* within the fashion industry for 40 years.

How excellent are you in your profession? Are you a capable leader within your profession or industry? And if not, you need to begin assessing how seriously you plan to compete in business because business will indeed spark competition. The most prepared and confident individuals and teams are those who acquire *adoration*, plan the most successful *presentations*, perform with *purpose*, and consistent *execution* toward their goal of *excellence*, the final element of the Gold Section.

But how many of you can honestly say that you have reached the point of *excellence* in your personal or company goals? And how would you rank your standings as compared to the *excellence* of the individuals and or companies within your field or industry?

Rank of Excellence
Please Consider Your Most Honest Mark Below

#1 / 1 out of 5 / 1 out of 10 / 1 out of 20 / 1 out of 50

Now we arrive at the most pivotal section on the text, the Green Section of *support*—the indisputable bridge of all success.

SUPPORT IS PIVOTAL

CHAPTER 17

THE DEFINITION OF SUPPORT

Without *support* and its most important Five Elements—as represented by the color green—there is no success in any business. *Support* is the steady bridge that takes us all where we want to go. It is symbolized by the image of a *straw basket* and the concept of public generosity. After we have all made the career decision to work hard with *passion* in the chosen occupation that we *love*, while mastering our specific *art*, *support* for our individual or company products and services is what we now all desire. We would all like to fill up our baskets, while forming strong teams of productive *execution*.

Webster's Third New International Dictionary has a multitude of definitions for *support*. In its many variations, to *support* is defined as to endure; to uphold by aid; to defend as valid; to argue in favor of; to vote for; to provide means; to give assistance to; to attend upon; to act with; to provide background; to pay the costs of; to provide a basis for the existence; and finally, to have or put into circulation enough money. Those are the supportive objectives of any and every business. So in this Green Section, we will now uncover our personal or company Representation of Support Number, or RSN.

While the components of *love* and *art* are exact numbers (100 percent and #1, respectively) there is no exact number that can be ascribed to *support*—or any exact approach to receive it. However, *support* of various forms must be received for there to be any economic progress in *love* for an *art*.

It is possible that you may hold false perceptions that make you more optimistic than honest concerning the *passion* you feel for your particular career or in your assessment of artistic *excellence* in the performance of that career. But when you indeed reach the pivotal component of *support*, the truth will be revealed. If no one else believes in your zeal or is willing to rank your skills as highly as you do, then you may need to reevaluate your honest assessments. The key to *support* is to make others—outside of yourself and your company—believe enough in your products and services to aid you in your goals.

The question of *support* becomes, *"How can we all manage to achieve success through the assistance, investment, and public favor of our ideas, products, services, knowledge, gifts, leadership, or overall character?"* Despite our beliefs in personal independence, no one is truly self-made without supportive measures from others. *Support* is what makes a society work. If no one ever supports anything, the society cannot progress.

How many houses have been built by just one person? How many people can teach themselves to build a house without guidance or training from someone else? How many people can produce all of the raw materials to build a house without trading with others? And even if one individual *could* execute all of the details of building a house, what good would that house then be if no one ever agreed to pay for it or live in it?

This is the condition of *love* and *art;* in the absence of *support* they do nothing. Achieving *support* from the individuals within a society is the most valuable goal in the human universe. Regardless of how highly we may think of our ourselves, our efforts, and our skills, without the validation of *support*, our personal assessments become meaningless in the world of business. Simply put, no *support* equals no *business*. So unless one is wealthy enough to live within a bubble of idle hobbies, the *purpose* of life in general is to produce objects that can be utilized for the survival, inspiration, and forward progress of living organisms.

In other words, what is the *purpose* of communal life if not to *support* others' goals, or to have your own goals supported? This important question remains a struggle of us all in business. And it must be answered before any successful enterprise can move forward. Therefore, we all forced to utilize our own methods to seek and find ways to fill up our *straw baskets*.

The public relations and media guru Mario Lavandeira, better known as Perez Hilton, understands the formula for amassing *support*. Known to millions as a celebrity gossip blogger, without his overwhelmingly supportive fan base, Perez Hilton would be just another fictitious name among millions. However, Lavandeira has developed his unique services and brand name into a worldwide business.

Love him or hate him, Perez Hilton has successfully turned celebrity news, views, and personal issues into his own creative form of entrepreneurship. He now attracts millions of international viewers to his PerezHilton.com web site each month, collecting hundreds of thousands of dollars in weekly advertising revenue.

While celebrity gossip may not sound like big business to you, consider the number of global newsstand magazines that have thrived or have folded in search of steady public readership. From *People* to *Vanity Fair*, and *Time* to *Playboy*, the periodical news, special interests, and gossip print industry continues to represent billions of dollars in advertising revenue, based solely on the demographics of a supportive readership. Corporations want to know *who* and *how many* loyal customers *support* each publication, so that they may decide *where* to invest their resources to attract a targeted audience.

Over the past decade—due to an increasingly competitive advertising field from the Internet, cable television networks, various new radio formats, and other forms of intellectual technology—many publications, including national newspapers, have suffered tremendous losses. Supporters of every vehicle are being stretched thin from far too many options. Nevertheless, those who stand out with the right formulas of *attraction* are still able to flourish, including Perez Hilton.

In a culture that worships instant information and immediate access to the inside scoop, be it on Madison Avenue, Wall Street, or Hollywood Boulevard, supported bloggers like Perez—who has been known to update as many as 20 blog posts per day—are making headway where more traditional media are faltering.

According to demographic research, PerezHilton.com scores above the Internet average with female viewers across the board, as well as with 18- to 34-year-olds, 35- to 49-year-olds, income groups of more than $100,000, and all nationalities. With his around-the-hour updates of gossip news information, his retention of repeated viewers has been nothing short of phenomenal, outmatching all similar websites by a nearly two to one ratio of monthly visits.

Many celebrities, whom Perez may have previously mocked on his website, now court him for photo opportunities to boost their own public profile through association. Specifically, in the music industry with mentioned music and spotlighted singles from YouTube, Perez's *support* of an unknown or favored artist has been able to send viewer numbers and fortunes soaring. Major music labels have even began to court Perez with conversations concerning his opinions and *support* of their new artists and music.

By consistently and fearlessly giving his viewers what they want in celebrity gossip, Perez Hilton has benefited from the power of *support*, by which he is able to successfully cross the bridge into legitimate and progressive enterprise. He has endured the hardships of competition, defended his base, argued in favor or against celebrities and their products, provided blog spotlights for the assistance of newcomers, and created a circulation of wealth from which to continue to *execute* the *love* for his *art*.

As I have often said on the lecture circuit when speaking about the successes of my own career, every entrepreneur and company must prepare themselves to market, promote, sell, and find the needed audience to continue their work, just as Mario Lavandeira and other successful entrepreneurs and winning companies have been able to do.

Each business must advance itself through the various cohesive networks that are built on efforts of others, just as Perez Hilton has done in tandem with friends, photographers, public relations reps, his lawyers, gossip associates, agents, event promoters, advertisers, sponsors, Internet technicians, search engine companies, and his supportive fan base of millions. It is all a concerted effort on which Lavandeira has been able to build a base of establishment. And as long as his PerezHilton.com is able to maintain or increase its numbers of viewers, Mario Lavandeira will remain a viable and successful businessman, whether we like it or not.

How many people *support* you or your company? How many customers utilize your products and services? The answer to those questions will predict the life or death of your business, no matter how much you claim to *love* it or how artistic you think you are. So no matter what your method of *execution*, find your most effective means of gathering *support*, and make sure you never forget to build it and maintain it in whatever you choose to do.

CHAPTER 18

WHY THE COLOR GREEN?

The color green is often used to represent nature. Organisms thrive when the land is green. It is the color that signifies a life that is ongoing and continuous. Green is synonymous with growth, potential, and development. To be considered green is to be new and workable, refreshing, pleasant, and lively. It is also the color of abundance, like a field of beautiful green grass, or the green vegetables that are healthy for our bodies.

To be without green is to be without life. The natural and needed component of *support* for our goals and endeavors is what gives us that life. An idea—like a plant—needs *green support* to grow. This is why the color green is the most pivotal section of *The Equation*. It represents the soil, sunlight, water, and vegetation of human ideas, services and products. Humans need economic, moral, and team *support* for their ideas to prosper within a community and beyond. So it is not by accident that American money is coded in greenbacks; nor is it an accident that a green light at an intersection means "Go." We have accepted the symbolic importance of green as the color-coded key of advancement.

It is also fair to state that no man has come to represent the color green in contemporary American society more than billionaire real-estate developer Donald J. Trump. Even before the popularity of his top-rated reality show, *The Apprentice*, the Trump name had become synonymous with wealth and property. Properties, like land, are best represented by the color green.

For more than 30 years, Donald Trump has worked tirelessly to amass the best real estate of green from which to build the grandest of human properties. Trump not only considers himself to be one of the best developers in the industry; he states it outright as an unabashed salesman. He effectively uses the story of his successes to generate public and investor trust that enables him to buy and build more properties. Green produces more green.

However, Trump is hardly a one-man operation. He understands that the development of any worthwhile real estate must combine the forces of various elements. There is the initial purchase of green land, the creation and financing of the architectural design, the raw materials to build it, construction and zoning of the building, and, finally, the marketing and resale of the completed property to guests, renters, and buyers. This completed process takes green, green, green, and *more* green—which means work, work, work, and *more* work. The completed and sold property will then need sufficient maintenance to hold its value.

Despite the amount of green that is available within a given society, the ability to acquire it is definitely not an easy task. If it were, then all entrepreneurs with *passion* and a great idea would attain it. And trust me when I tell you that they don't.

Mr. Trump—highlighting his own abilities to continuously fill up his *green baskets* of *support*-decided to write a bestselling book on the subject, *The Art of the Deal* (1987). Ironically, Trump used the word *art*, as well as the symbol of gold, realizing that there is a competitive *skill* involved in gathering green. In order to build *support*, the public must believe that the green is good. Obviously, through his many years of quality goods, salesmanship, and swagger, Donald J. Trump has been able to gain the *support* and recognition of millions of followers, who believe in his public record, his philosophy, his advice, and his deals.

The color green is indeed the Trump color. The unabashed entrepreneur has been known to pitch the value of his hair, his homes, his wives, his children, his politics, his personal opinions, and his grand ideas to millions of supporters who have found his advise to be bold, interesting, and inspirational. With his continued use of strong public imagery and ostentatious flair, Trump has continued to close lucrative deals with the *support* of investors, including international moguls, while he continues to increase his public fan base.

With an estimated net worth of $3 billion, Trump has never been the richest or most successful man in the world. But you would never know it from listening to him. Trump has established a long track record of speaking about his business experiences with confidence and energy, as though he were the wealthiest, most intelligent, and successful deal maker who has ever lived. How else could he lure millions of visitors, guests, gamblers, partners, financiers, executives, and viewers to *support* his hotels, casinos, resorts, condominiums, beauty pageants, publications, and television programs?

Even the most passionate of red and gifted of gold can be losers without the necessary green. Donald Trump was forced to learn that fact the hard way for himself. When he overextended his resources—as ambitious men have been known to do—the level of unwavering *support* he maintained from bankers, partners, private investors, and family members was strong enough to convince them all to ride through the hard times with him, as he remained intent upon and confident in rebuilding his empire of real estate. And through *support*, he was able to succeed in rebuilding his wealth and image on more than one occasion.

As with Enzo Ferrari's passionate red, and Oscar De La Hoya's talented gold, the Donald J. Trump brand has created the expanding green of prosperity. He has utilized his complete showmanship as a necessary means of acquiring and maintaining wealth. So whether one has to look good; smell good; talk big, bad and bold; be nice, be mean, be interesting; know all the right people; come from the right family; graduate from the right schools; make a million phones calls; hire the right team; create the greatest marketing plan; or know all the right information—the individual, community and company deals of *support* must be closed for business. There is no successful business without the imperative process of filling up *green baskets*.

To gain *support*, a business person and or company must have *attraction, packaging, organization*, and *imagery* that produces *movement*. These are The Five Elements of Support. *Support* must grow for any business idea to survive. And that *support* is best represented by the color green.

CHAPTER 19

ATTRACTION

Webster's Third New International Dictionary defines the word *attraction* as: a characteristic that elicits interest or admiration; an attracting quality. *Attraction* belongs to people who possess magnetic charm. It is a force that draws oppositely magnetized bodies together and compels them to resist their separation. *Attraction* is also the action or power of extracting a response—a quality that fascinates people by appealing to their desires and tastes. And finally, *attraction* is defined as a person, thing, or performance that attracts crowds.

Attraction is the first important element of *support*. Before people are willing to aid, vote for, give assistance to, buy, or utilize the services or products of an individual or company, that individual or company must attract them first. *Attraction* is why I chose Perez Hilton and Donald J. Trump as representations of what it means to seek and acquire *green support*. Both individuals have used the necessary law of *attraction* to spark, maintain, and grow their respective businesses. And if you or your company lacks the ingredients of interest, admiration, and magnetism to bring bodies together that resist separation from your goods, then you may need to consider how you might go about acquiring them.

Richard Branson, the British entrepreneur and founder of the Virgin Group—a conglomerate of various international businesses—has used a bold and brash method of *attraction* to build one of the most successful and recognized company brands in the world. His various Virgin enterprises have thrived, failed, and thrived again through his top-to-bottom beliefs in optimism and adventure. By living out an excitable and public lifestyle, Branson has been able to create not only interest in his businesses, but worldwide admiration for his go-for-it-all character.

Regardless of how we may feel about over-the-top personalities, the winning charm and infatuation of character allows individuals to attract wonder and notice—not only from the public, but among wealthy investors who recognize the extreme importance of learning how to stand out in a crowd. Any investor who recognizes and admires your personal or company appeal is a lot more likely to consider the *support* of your business.

Branson, born in South London in 1950, suffered from dyslexia and poor academic marks in grade school. Nevertheless, by the time he had turned 16, he had already started three separate businesses, succeeding with his third effort, a magazine entitled *Student*, with a circulation of 50,000 copies that was published out of a London basement. As a high school dropout and budding entrepreneur, Branson had to attract young, innovative hard workers to join him in his early publishing and distribution efforts. And he did.

He and his loyal teammates were then able to develop a mail order record company in 1969, which led to the forming of his Virgin company brand of music and megastores in the 1970s. The growing enterprise called "Virgin"—a play on words to describe the new music the young partners sold, as well as to reflect on their new experiences within the business world—became an attractive company catch name. After opening a London-based record shop, Branson went on to form Virgin Records with partner Nick Powell. The upstart label also established a recording studio for artists, becoming a hub for the varied musical talents of Mike Oldfield.

With the combination of Virgin record stores, and the first recorded release from the Virgin label—Mike Oldfield's *Tubular Bells*—Branson and his partner had produced a British chart topper, which helped the label to attract and sign the controversial, and soon-to-be-legendary, Sex Pistols.

Continuing in their goals of innovation and competitive challenges, the Virgin Record group won praise for exposing the public to new forms of music and new bands, including the wildly popular music of Culture Club, while supporting the changing nightclub scene. Branson and his partners were never afraid to try new ideas, taking successful risks that sparked the imagination of a worldwide following.

As the accomplishments of his music label and the business success of Virgin Megastores blossomed during the 1980s, Branson leaped headfirst into the airline business, forming Virgin Atlantic Airways in 1984. Going against the grain of the naysayers, who called his airline idea madness, Branson led his Virgin Group to establish a flamboyant and competitive airline for international travel, known for fair prices and quality service.

Not stopping there, Branson soon found himself taking up the challenge of breaking and setting individual world travel records. With record-setting treks across the Atlantic and Pacific Oceans in boats and in hot air balloons, Branson became a spectacle to the world. Next, he attempted to circumnavigate the globe, as the world watched, waited, listened, and asked themselves the question, "Is this rich man crazy or what?"

Nevertheless, Branson's adventurous antics kept everyone's attention, as his popularity and business ventures expanded worldwide. Branson launched his Virgin Group brand into such business enterprises as mobile telephones, railways, cruise lines, vodka, publishing, technology, friendly fuels, media, world charity, human development think tanks, soccer teams, and galactic space travel.

Yes, you read that correctly, Richard Branson wants to fly Virgin customers into outer space, utilizing a Spaceship One technology that was initially funded by Microsoft co-founder Paul Allen, and designed by aeronautical engineer and visionary Burt Rutan. Virgin Galactic plans to makes its first space flight tickets available to the public by late 2009, with an estimated starting price of $200,000. With Branson's track record of a daring, world-wide marketing style, we can all expect to hear plenty about his space travel ideas and goals in 2009.

An admitted thrill-seeker and adrenalin junkie—now at age 58—Branson claims his business philosophy is all about having fun and having the gall to take the necessary risks involved in entrepreneurship, which includes becoming a public personality. Give the people something to enjoy, to imagine, to strive for, and to talk about. Richard Branson does it all well, and he sees no reason to slow down. He's having far too much fun keeping up with the changing trends of international enterprise.

When you talk about the law of *attraction* in business, Branson is way ahead of the pack. His Virgin Group remains as one of the top three favorite and most respected companies in the UK, and his creative force of visionaries have established more than 200 independently run entities around the world. With an estimated fortune of $8 billion, Branson has obviously succeeded in attracting plenty of worldwide supporters.

However, the element of *attraction* includes more than just the magnetism of one particular person or company. The various methods of *attraction* are utilized daily to elicit a response from people in a multitude of industries. When we talk about appealing to people's desires and tastes, the words *advertisement, promotion, marketing, public relations, commercials,* and *endorsements* all come to mind. These tools are all utilized through the media of television, radio, newspapers, magazines, and the Internet: as well as through the public and private spaces of highway billboards, interiors and exteriors of buildings, trains and train stations, buses and bus stops, airports and airplanes, concert halls and stadiums, and many other public and private spaces.

Promotion, promotion, promotion to attract is very important. This is the stage of business where many modest, hesitant, and insecure people become overwhelmed and disillusioned. They soon begin to ask, "Why do I have to promote so much? If the people like it, they like it, and if they don't, they don't." Experienced business people respond, "First of all, the people need to *know* about the product, and we can never *assume* that they already do. So, however we need to get the word out, we must *do it;* and do it *successfully."* If people don't do this, how serious can they be about the success of their business.

As a professional in the book publishing industry, my own methods of *attraction* were my boundless energy, a positive attitude, and my youth. At age 23, my ability to publish and sell books was a novelty. I was also easy on the eyes for a majority of women readers who supported adult fiction.

As superficial as it may sound to some, looks are a major part of *attraction*, in *everything*. So I went out and bought new suits, ties, shirts, sports jackets, and anything that made me look more striking to a supportive crowd. But the thing I used the most was my mouth. I learned to keep it running. And if I couldn't count on the media to find me, I could surely count on myself to step up and make myself heard and noticed.

In this Green Section, it becomes imperative to attract the strongest or widest audience of supporters possible. As Richard Branson would tell us, we must all learn to use whatever advantages of character, personality, interests, or unique abilities that we possess in our favor. And as with any business plan, you must make sure that you keep an accurate account of your true number of supporters, and remember to treat them well. So with realistic supportive numbers in mind, what range of people are you able to honestly attract to *support* the personal goals of your career, or the services and products of your company?

The Attraction Chart
Please Consider Your Most Honest Mark Below

Communal — Local — Regional — National — World

Communal refers to thousands of supporters or less in any given community. *Local* refers to hundreds of thousands of supporters within a localized area. *Regional* refers to millions of supporters in a given region. *National* refers to tens of millions of supporters around a nation. And *world* refers to hundreds of millions of supporters around the globe.

Which range of supporters have you or your company been able to attract through radio, television, print, Internet, public relations, promotions, events, or old-fashioned word-of-mouth concerning your talent, services, or products? If you have not attempted or succeeded in appealing to a given audience to *support* your efforts, now you know you have work to do. And in the final section, "The Equation in Use," you may continue to fill in your chart accordingly.

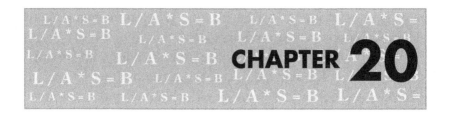

CHAPTER 20

PACKAGING

It was a bit of a challenge for me to define *packaging* using just one source. In *Webster's Third New International Dictionary*, the word *package* is defined—for business purposes—as a combination of related elements to be accepted or rejected as a whole; a combination of benefits; or, a combination of necessaries. I used these definitions and a perusal through the *Dictionary of Business Terms*—where packaging was defined as a package deal, or a comprehensive plan or proposition for marketing—to create one, coherent meaning for our purposes.

Basically, *packaging* is all about giving customers deals on related products and services that they will find too irresistibly priced to turn down. In other words: if consumers are hesitant to buy Product A alone, then offer them Product A and B at a discounted rate. If the customer remains hesitant, then throw in Product C for good measure. Once you have gained a new customer as a supporter of your products and services, make sure you offer them your next line of goods to continue their *support*.

The most basic and everyday packaged deal that comes to mind for me is McDonald's Happy Meal. If you have ever been around a group of hungry kids, the combination of a hamburger, fries, a drink, and a toy, all packaged inside a kid-friendly box, is a wonderful thing to have. And the price for the package has always been lower than buying each item individually. In fact, the toy—usually a licensed character from a recent children's movie—is basically thrown in for free. The purpose of the toy is to lock in the *loyalty* of young kids, who will be hungry for more food and another toy in the future.

McDonald's Happy Meal is the simplest and most ingenious *packaging* concept in the world. It compels parents to spend their money on impulse—at the incessant request of their children. Nearly every other fast food and family restaurant was then forced to offer packaged deals of their own to compete, as well as amusements parks, trade shows, and movie theaters. *Packaging* a valuable discount to families of four, five and sometimes six members, allows a company to sell more product while building more loyal customers all at once. The alternative of selling one item to one customer at a time would amount to a very long, tedious and possibly failed execution of business.

I learned the power of *packaging* early on in my own book publishing experiences more than a dozen years ago. The basic rule is to sell more product to more people in the fewest transactions. Group sales trump individual sales. That's just smart business if your goals is to move volumes of product. So as soon as I had two $12.95, soft-cover books to sell, I offered them both at book events at two for $20, plus my autographed signature, with whatever you wanted me to write in the book. The simple math, plus the personal touch of good customer service, allowed me to move twice as many books at a $3 discount to the customer. But I didn't mind giving a $3 discount if I could sell my books faster. Moving the product was my goal. And if you can find a way to move more of your product without the added expense of advertising, then do it.

Packaging is not only about making a profit; it's actually a built-in form of promotion. The faster you can sell your goods to more people, the easier it is to validate the quality of your business. In other words, you want more people to experience what you have to offer, and you're prepared to give them a sample of it at a discounted price to do so. You then allow the satisfied customers to do the talking for you through word of mouth. But there is no word of mouth if customers don't have the product. So give them the product.

Endorsement deals are another form of *packaging* as a combination of benefits. A company benefits by linking itself up with a popular personality, who is paid a fee for their attachment to the product, while appearing in promotions that enhance the value of both parties. In this situation, the public gets to buy a quality product enhanced by their favorite personality. An endorsement package is also a way in which new products are promoted, by association with a trusted brand name.

The *packaging* of a trusted brand name in combination with related goods brings to mind the very strong impact of entrepreneur Martha Stewart. Born Martha Helen Kostyra of Polish-American parents, Martha has been firmly established as the most popular homemaking, cooking, decorating, and merchandising brand, with an influence on the personal tastes of women everywhere.

After years of being an active straight-A student with a multitude of interests and talents that included modeling, gardening, art, writing, chemistry, architecture, and history, Martha married Andrew Stewart in 1961. Having her first and only child—a daughter Alexis in 1965—Stewart became a stockbroker in 1967. She later returned to life at home in 1973, when she and her husband moved into a massive farmhouse in Connecticut. Their restoration and decoration of the new home spawned her creative talents, and eventually became the background set for the *Martha Stewart Living* television program.

In 1976, Martha started a catering business with modeling friend Norma Collier. She then bought out Collier's portion of the business, managed a successful gourmet food store, and developed a cookbook with recipes and photos from her catered parties. The cookbook would become the *New York Times* 1977 bestseller *Entertaining*, which Stewart wrote with ghostwriter Elizabeth Hayes.

Stewart's first successful book spawned several other books that followed throughout the 1980s. She was once again able to utilize her writing skills by penning newspaper columns and magazine articles—many of which were pieces on homemaking. And her numerous appearances on television included *The Oprah Winfrey Show*.

Time Publishing Ventures eventually developed the *Martha Stewart Living* magazine in 1990, for which Stewart served as the editor in chief. The magazine led to the creation of her popular television show of the same name. As she continued to develop herself as a recognizable brand, *New York Magazine* soon declared her "the definitive American woman of our time."

In 1999, Stewart took her company public with business partner Sharon Patrick, naming it Martha Stewart Living Omnimedia. The Martha Stewart brand includes home and garden, recipes and cooking; arts, crafts and merchandising; television and publishing; website and online services; and more.

The popular brand of Martha Stewart is now one of the most obvious case studies of successful *packaging*. After enduring a 2004 conviction and prison sentence for several federal business-related charges, Stewart returned to the public business world less than a year later with her company still intact. Upon her release from prison, she presented new ideas for her clothing line, performed plenty of media interviews, and was offered a new television show, *The Apprentice: Martha Stewart* by the one and only Donald J. Trump.

Valued at more than half a billion dollars to date, the Martha Stewart empire continues to grow. And like the various articles of clothing and accessories that come together to make a proper outfit, certain groups of items are comparable and complementary. The combination of various skills, hobbies, products, and services all associated with the *packaging* of one woman, are what made the name and business of Martha Stewart so powerful. Finding a family of ideas, people, places, foods, products, and services that you can group collectively in one big deal will often make the business execution easier to accomplish. So if millions of American women are familiar with the Martha Stewart brand for one successful item, they definitely can—and likely will—become familiar with her for another.

Ultimately, the efforts applied in gaining business *support* from a loyal customer base are all up to you. Good business people have found that combining relatable goods and services into a packaged and feasible price has worked—time and time again—at developing successful sales methods, while building valuable customer relationships. So if you are serious about the success of your business, then how often have you earnestly offered a packaged deal with valuable links to the skills, products, and services that you offer? Your honesty will move you forward in recognizing what you need to do in order to inspire positive changes.

 ## The Packaging Chart
Please Consider Your Most Honest Mark Below

Communal—Local—Regional—National—World

You will create very long days, weeks, months, and years for yourself, your company, and your employees if you attempt to sell one item at a time. So if you need to package several items together at a lower price, or introduce your new items through established ones, then by all means *do it*. Give your customer something of extra value as an add-in, or link-up with people who are already popular and who fit the audience and image of your product or company. You owe it to your business to make those deals happen; otherwise be prepared to suffer the consequences.

Retail stores are known to push buy-one, get-one-free deals for a reason. They're trying to *move* the product. Plain and simple. And if you never knew the meaning or full power of *packaging* before—now you know. In the final section, "The Equation in Use," you may continue to fill in your chart.

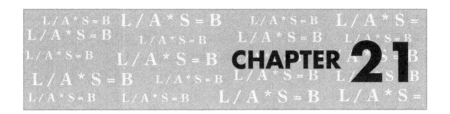

CHAPTER 21

ORGANIZATION

Webster's Third New International Dictionary defines the word *organization* as the act or process of organizing; the unification and harmonizing of all elements of a work of art; and a group of people who have a more or less constant membership, with a body of officers, a purpose and a usual set of regulations. *Organization* is also defined as a state or manner of being organized, with purposeful and systematic arrangement, including the established relationships of personnel through lines of authority and responsibility with delegated and assigned duties.

In business an *organization* often refers to a team, which would include any group of managers, lawyers, publicists, marketers, accountants, agents, assistants, salespeople, secretaries, and other colleagues or teammates. Depending on your field, you can include other positions as necessary. However, the term *organization* not only includes the work of bringing the elements of business into harmony, but more importantly, bringing the working groups of *people* into harmony.

When it comes to the element of *organization*, many individual artists and entrepreneurs—no matter how successful—have faced their share of difficulty. The problem is often the result of a lack of communication, trust, capital, regularity, and the *execution* of goals and ideas. Basically, to be successful as a team, an *organization* must have a workable plan, structure, and paid professionals who understand and can carry out their designed goals.

A company may hold a board meeting to discuss plans of *execution* toward their goals. At the end of such a meeting, the CEO will make the final decision, and the managers will dictate duties to the staff—with no ifs, ands, or buts. Whoever does not execute will have to answer to a team supervisor, who will report to a higher manager, who then answers to the vice president, CEO, or owner of the company.

Within this form of regimented hierarchy, the top artists—or CEOs—are isolated from much of the chaos at the bottom. This organizational structure is set up through a delegation of staff. This creates two possible reactions from the top down—a sense of harmony or a sense of panic. Harmony gets the job done with poise. Panic can lead to failure. But like it or not, this top-to-bottom power structure allows the team members to accept their positions, and carry out their necessary duties—or else.

The problem with many individual artists—including lower-level entrepreneurs—is the lack of understanding, tolerance, and desire to work within this chain of command. Other problems include lack of necessary staff and capital to set the *organization* into place. Running an organized and productive office is a challenging task, which requires talent, along with the right mix of philosophy, system, and people.

An individual artist and entrepreneur who was able to pull together an extremely successful *organization* was Berry Gordy III, founder and CEO of the legendary Motown Records company of the 1960s and 1970s. Born in 1929, right before the depression of the 1930s, Gordy's family of 10 lost their home and subsisted on welfare in a two-story, rat-infested shack on the west side of Detroit.

Berry Gordy's father then came up with an idea—based on his own father's observation of the South—that no matter what, "people have to eat." So he took over a small, failing grocery store on the east side of Detroit and managed to turn it into a profit-making venture. The Gordy clan became one of the only African-American families to own commercial property in Detroit—a position that would teach a young entrepreneur all about the importance of hard work, family unity, and confident leadership.

Under his father's watchful eye, Berry Gordy III would soon learn the necessary skills of management, negotiating prices, staying busy, and making a profit—all lessons that would become apparent in Gordy's future as a successful executive in the music industry.

However, Gordy was not particularly focused on school or on making a serious living like his siblings, and he dropped out in the eleventh grade to pursue his interest in boxing—partly in admiration for the career of Joe Louis. Gordy had high hopes of striking it rich in a hurry. But after a marginally successful career as a boxer, he was drafted into the United States Army in 1950 for the Korean War, which put his championship ambitions on hold.

Berry Gordy returned from Korea in 1953, married his first wife, and revisited another early interest, music and song writing. He had loved music and dabbled in it since childhood. He developed and wrote songs for a few years, and eventually opened the 3-D Record Mart—a record store featuring jazz music—before the business shut down.

After his setback, Gordy found work at the Michigan auto plants to make ends meet. His family then managed to help him make contact with music legend Al Green—an introduction that led to a chance meeting with singer Jackie Wilson. In 1957, Wilson recorded *Rete Petite*—a song that Gordy had co-written with his sister Gwen and sidekick, Billy Davis. The song became a modest hit, and Wilson went on to record four more songs co-written by Gordy over the next several years.

Remembering the lessons of budgets and business that he had learned as an adolescent, Gordy reinvested his song earnings—along with an $800 family loan—into producing music, writing songs, and finding talented performers of his own. Soon afterward, he established Motown Records—named after

Detroit's popularity as the Motor City—where Gordy was ready to put into effect all of his acquired knowledge about organized business.

Operating under the notion that the automobile assembly line could be applied to the music industry, Berry Gordy put everyone he could find to work—including his second wife, family members, friends, and every talented musician or performer he could find. From there, Gordy designed what he called a hit factory—or Hitsville U.S.A.—a program in search of talented, raw, young performers that he could mold into professional entertainers for the nation at large. In addition to creating hits that included both meaningful soul music and catchy songs that had universal appeal, Gordy was strongly advised to set up an Artist Development Department. Also known as the company "charm school," this *organization* taught performers how to sing, dance, stand, sit, dress, and carry themselves like honorable professionals in the public.

Gordy utilized knowledgeable veterans, as well as his skilled family members, to teach his young team of performers the basics and beyond: how to play the music, choreograph dance steps, greet television and stage hosts, and respond to their new fan base and popularity. Gordy also wrote some of his own songs, collaborated on many others, and put together the best songwriters and set musicians to compete with each other for the hottest melodies, hooks, singles, and ideas.

This so-called charm school of artist development was in step with Gordy's grand scheme of creating an organized business within the music industry. The business of entertainment was about more than just singing, dancing, and making music; a winning formula of stage presence and overall *execution* had to planned, orchestrated, and presented in an organized fashion to create a system of success. And that's exactly what Gordy's Motown machine was able to do.

As Motown Records set the nation on fire, money and esteem began to roll in from hit after hit; and once again, Berry Gordy bore in mind his father's many lessons about business. The Motown system of hit making had to continue like any other business.

So Gordy kept his performers and musicians busy despite their overwhelming success. He instinctively understood that the system of hit making could not allow economically and emotionally fulfilled artists to slow down. With too many great songs, great music, and great Motown moments to name, Gordy had no choice but to remain above it all as a crafty and driven executive—who was always several steps ahead of everyone.

With a young Smokey Robinson, Marvin Gaye, Diana Ross, Stevie Wonder, Mary Wells, Gladys Knight, Michael Jackson, Rick James, the Funk Brothers, Holland-Dozier-Holland, and the many other young and volatile performers who made up the members of the Supremes, the Temptations, the Miracles, the Vandellas, the Contours, the Jackson 5, the Pips—and all of the lesser-known performers and band members, Berry Gordy III definitely had his hands full. However, Gordy was able to maintain order long enough to turn his talented performers and musicians into legends.

By the time the Motown family began to fall apart in the mid 1970s—with plenty of ill will from artists toward the man who had created the organized business model that brought them all fame—Berry Gordy shifted his fast-moving gears again. He negotiated his way into the film world—arranging a classic soundtrack for *Cooley High* and producing the hit films *Lady Sings the Blues*, *Mahogany*, and *The Last Dragon*.

With his talented team of maturing performers defecting fast to other record labels for independence and huge pay days, Gordy moved Motown to Los Angeles and eventually sold the company for a reported $61 million dollars and change in 1988. He managed, however, to retain a large chunk of the music's publishing rights, which will continue to pay him huge dividends from one of the largest and most successful song libraries in music history.

It's incredible to think that Berry Gordy was able to keep all of that amazing talent under one organized roof for so long. In today's industry of free agency and bidding wars, it has become increasingly difficult to hold together any talented team, let alone manage multiple groups of superstars. So despite the disgruntled reports about his unfair business practices, each and every one of us would have to ask ourselves, "How would I have been able to hold that same incredible group of talented people together to create what Berry Gordy did?"

I know all about the difficulties of building a successful team myself. For most of my own business career, I have been a do-it-yourselfer, who has preferred small groups over large ones. Basically, I have been a one-man wrecking crew from start to finish: writing, typesetting, legalizing company names, setting up bank accounts, gathering information, negotiating funding, paying for outside services, making all the phone calls; carrying, storing, and shipping boxes of books; setting up distribution and meeting with book store managers, newspaper editors, and radio talk show hosts. I even wrote up my own consignment papers while collecting all of the checks. So if you were to ask me about the *organization* of publishing a book, I would have it all down to a science. But as I have stated at the beginning of this Green Section of *support*, one man or woman cannot execute all of the needed elements of a successful and growing *business*.

That's not to say it's a bad idea to get up and do what you need to do when you need to do it. However, I had gotten so used to doing everything on my own, that I found myself unable to even *attempt* much delegation. And a lot of it had to do with accountability. Within any *organization*, you must find professionals who are capable and willing to carry out your business goals and needs—consistently. Those individuals need to be recruited, convinced, empowered, trusted, and secured through a salary or through normal business practices.

The ability to select and retain the needed professionals to form a successful business team becomes a skill in itself. A team must then be positioned, inspired, trained, cultivated, and led to move toward the achievement of individual and company goals. However, the more time one person spends doing 20 different tasks, the less diversity of professionalism and exercise of leadership can be devoted to team success.

One of many observations Berry Gordy made in his own organizational structure and management style was that he selected people over positions. In other words, he saw it as more important to select quality people and to place them in the best positions to succeed, rather than force himself to fill positions with the wrong people to execute the company mission. So Gordy built his staff, loaded with more malleable talent who could adapt to the team mission, rather than hire rigid specialists who could not.

Another very successful *organization* that utilizes the people-over-position model is the global cosmetic brand Mary Kay. Touting the Golden Rule—"Do unto others as you would have them do unto you"—Mary Kay Ash, a Texas-born saleswoman, went on to establish one of strongest direct sales industries in the world, which to this day is run exclusively through individual sales agents.

Ash spent over 30 years working for several direct sales companies. From 1930 to 1960, she honed her skills as a salesperson and trainer. But she retired in 1963, frustrated by her inability to advance in companies that gave promotions to men. Ash had built an incredible team of a 150 salespeople under her wing at Stanley Home Products. However, instead of receiving accolades from the company for whom she worked on a team—commission basis—Ash was reassigned in an attempt to diminish her influence, profits, and impact on the company. So she decided to retire, and wrote her self-titled book—*Mary Ash*—to assist women in business.

The book went on to become a national bestseller that was published in several languages. In 1963, the year of the book's publication, Mary Kay and her son, Richard Rogers, began Mary Kay Cosmetics with a $5,000 investment. They operated from a storefront in Dallas under the philosophy that praising people leads to success. Mary Kay Ash soon became nationally known for awarding pink Cadillacs to her top salespeople as a visible token of their success. And to this day her book continues to serve as a business plan for the company.

Mary Kay's marketing plan was based on the notion that she could best help women to advance by helping others to succeed. Therefore, each saleswoman who built a successful team would receive a portion of her team's commission. She also advised her saleswomen to honor "God first, family second, career third." She encouraged them to allow their intellect to rely on their instincts, break down the barriers to success by creating new directions, and make sure that they always followed through on their plans.

Following a chance 1979 television interview with CBS's 60 *Minutes*—an interview that showed the team lessons, rules, goals and slogans all in place—the Mary Kay company exploded with popularity and *support*.

For her successful *execution* in business leadership, Mary Kay has been awarded countless awards from business groups—including the prestigious Horatio Alger Award— and was inducted into the Junior Achievement U.S. Business Hall of Fame in 1996. A Mary Kay Ash Charitable Foundation was established in her name to raise money to combat domestic violence and cancers affecting women. And by the time of her death in November of 2001, Ash had written two additional best selling business books: *Mary Kay on People Management* (1984) and *You Can Have it All* (1995). Both works portrayed her industrious wisdom— material that the renowned Harvard Business School included in their courses.

To date, Mary Kay Inc.—which is still run by Ash's son Richard Rogers—has become a multibillion-dollar brand with close to two million employees and outlets in more than 30 countries around the world.

Now that's *organization!* If only we could all find enthusiastic and driven people to order and resell our products around the nation and the world—then we could *all* become successful in business. A quality team that is able to execute from the same page of business, will most likely achieve more consistent success than a single genius. However, some of us are able to organize a talented group to do so, while others are not. But what we all have to realize is that even extreme talents need *support* for their work to have long-term value. An *organization* is imperative for broader success in business.

To succeed within an ongoing industry, the examples of Berry Gordy and Mary Kay Ash—who surrounded themselves with the best people within a workable system—shows us just a few of the many ways to develop a successful team unit. So ask yourself honestly, what segments of the population have you or your company been able to attract through your teamwork, *organization*, or the structure of your business?

The Organization Chart
Please Consider Your Most Honest Mark Below

Communal—Local—Regional—National—World

If you are still learning the hard lessons about *organization* and attempting to find business teammates that you can trust, pay fairly, count on, and succeed with, then you know now like I know how very important the element is in industry. And as the saying goes, "Knowing is half the battle."

I am definitely at work on improving my organizational habits and needs toward achieving greater success. Great examples and information about successful managing methods that fit our business models, as well as individual and company personalities are all around us. But it's up to all of us to do what we need to do to improve our weaknesses and turn them into strengths. So as I presently seek the knowledge, the teammates, and the practice to move toward my goals, what are you now prepared to do to improve your organizational needs?

In the final section, "The Equation in Use," you must continue to be honest. If your *organization* is already in place and you're ready to rock and roll with successful *execution*, then I honestly envy you, and I hope to join you shortly with my own accountable team.

CHAPTER 22

IMAGERY

Webster's Third New International Dictionary defines the word *imagery* as "the product of image makers; the art of making images and image worship." *Imagery* is also described as "an ornate or heightened description or figures of speech; the often peculiarly individual concrete or figurative diction used by a writer in those portions of his text where he wishes to produce a particular effect." The word also refers to the mental images and products of the imagination.

When we speak of *imagery* as heightened descriptions, figures of speech, or diction used by a writer to produce a particular effect, the classic works of William Shakespeare come to mind. In elaborate stage plays, worldwide, the many works of Shakespeare have continued to be relevant in the world's artistic culture. So does the speech, diction, images, and heightened effects of business.

Every industry and art form has its own stylized vocabulary, *imagery*, and language. The image of a suit, tie, briefcase, and an office building alone have all become synonymous with the seriousness of business enterprise around the world. The importance of specific *imagery* implanted in the human mind helps to create memory recall. Specific terms and images allow us all to lock the goals and purposes of certain individuals, enterprises, and companies in mind and recognize them immediately when we see or hear about them again. Therefore, those who are serious about gaining and keeping public *support* for their businesses have learned to continue pushing the specific language, *imagery*, and goals of their products and services to create an accepted and recognizable brand.

The push of frequent brand *imagery* is where heavy company marketing comes into play. With the *packaging* of television, radio, print advertisement, and, most recently, the Internet for public marketing, the more the mind is able to see, hear, and become familiar with the same object, logo, jingle, voice, character, message, or even a particular sound or color, the more the mind will readily accept it.

Worldwide *imagery* and branding have become a tremendous influence on what we deem as attractive, familiar, and ultimately desirable. Whenever a visual object or an identifiable image of any form becomes familiar to us, we are more likely to fall in line to *support* the things that are associated with it. The *support* of certain products associated with an image and brand becomes normal behavior. You simply get used to it. And when the public becomes weary of it, the determined individuals, companies, and brands try to modify their images, create new ones, or push new products and services that reinforce their brands all over again.

Through the creation of mental images and products of the imagination, few brands have inspired the evocative *imagery* of the Cadillac. Whether it's the lineage of the cars themselves, which dates back to the early 1900s—when the Cadillac brand was formed from the remnants of The Henry Ford company—or their racy new commercials featuring the slogan—"Life. Liberty. And The Pursuit."—Cadillacs are known worldwide for their luxury, classiness, and overall extravagance. Symbolized by the emblem of a colorful shield enclosed within a silver reef, the Cadillac automobile has captured the imagination of millions of car enthusiasts for more than a hundred years.

Dreamed up in 1902, when auto engineer Henry M. Leland convinced William Murphy and Lemuel Bowen—key Ford company partners—to continue business in the automobile industry, using Leland's one-cylinder engine, the Cadillac was born. Named after the French explorer Antoine Laumet de La Mothe, sieur de Cadillac, who founded Detroit in 1701, Cadillac helped define advanced engineering, wealth, and style in early automotive history. A leader of many firsts in the industry, including the first manufacturer to release cars with a fully enclosed cab as factory equipment, the first to incorporate an electrical system consisting of cranking, lighting, and ignition, the first to regulate engine cooling by thermostat, the first to offer an electric starter, the first to commission artist-influenced body designs, the first to use shatter-resistant glass, the first to design a fully synchronized manual transition, and the first to produce and utilize a V8 engine.

Purchased by the General Motors corporation in 1909, the Cadillac would maintain its *imagery* of first-class luxury and become one of the world's finest-made vehicles. Becoming known for its large and ostentatious front chrome grille and Dagmar bumpers, Cadillac aimed ultra-exclusive luxury cars at an upper-class market, in competition with such well-built and powerful models as the Pierce-Arrow and the Duesenberg. The company added 12- and 16-cylinder engines of high power, smoothness, and quietness, encased in custom coach-built bodies.

One of the first high-end companies to advocate advertising to African-American customers, Cadillac became a chosen and loyal brand of style and stature not only among the wealthy, but within the urban communities of blue collar workers. Surviving through World Wars, depressions, auto industry competition, and increases in gas prices, the Cadillac brand produced record sales in the 1970s with the increasing popularity of the DeVille and Eldorado models that would take the brand to new heights in the public arena. The Cadillac style was seemingly *everywhere!*

By the 1980s, the Cadillac name, emblem, brand, and *imagery* was casually associated with everything of value. Even the Rolex watch company—no stranger to luxury—began to coin its products as "the Cadillac of watches." But as the Cadillac brand and image continued to dominate—while introducing smaller, fuel-saving models—its powerful force of association of style and class influenced the General Motors Company to create several look-a-like models from its other divisions that served to cripple Cadillac's hold on the luxury auto market.

In the 1990s, with steep competition from Lincoln, Mercedes Benz, BMW, Lexus, and Acura, Cadillac made several attempts to reclaim its prominence, including the introduction of the convertible Allante, designed in Italy. An eventual failure—along with the downsized models of the Seville, the Cimarron, and the Catera—Cadillac finally struck gold again with its introduction of the Escalade SUV in the late 1990s. However—while competing with the Ford Explorer, the Lincoln Navigator, and a horde of other sport utility vehicles from every car company—Cadillac was not able to reclaim its once celebrated luster and leadership in automobile industry. Nevertheless, the Cadillac name and emblem continue to spark the imagination as a fine example of just how powerful a brand and image can be.

Those of us who are old enough to begin to think of Cadillac as an image and brand of the past can now begin to think of the international city of Dubai as an image and brand of the *future*. The second-largest and most populated emirate of the seven that comprise the United Arab Emirates (UAE) in the Middle East, the Dubai government's decision to diversify from an oil-reliant economy to one that is service- and tourism-oriented, has made real estate and development more valuable, and turned the nation into one of the fastest-growing cities in the world.

A multi-cultural nation, with a high quality of life for people to live and work, as well as a tourism destination, 75 percent of Dubai's population of nearly a million people are expatriates from over 185 nationalities.

With an award-wining Emirates Airline, an ultramodern airport that handles nearly 14 million passengers, and flights to over 140 destinations annually, Dubai is the home of the world's first seven-star hotel—the Burj Al Arab—with many more on the way. Presently boasting one of the largest shopping malls in the Middle East, with an indoor ski lodge—Ski Dubai—the emirate is currently the third-largest re-export center in the world, with state-of-the-art medical and educational facilities. It is also host of the Dubai World Cup—the world's richest horse race—and host of world-class business forums and a month-long shopping festival.

Dubai has earned its reputation as a preeminent commercial center with an innovative, dynamic, and entrepreneurial business culture. Strategically located at the center of trade and commerce between the nations of Eastern Asia and Western Europe, as well as a midpoint between Africa and India, Dubai is politically stable, progressive, and pro-business, with a highly developed commitment to private enterprise. Business-friendly regulations and highly favorable taxes and customs have allowed the nation to attract investors from all over the world in every industry.

However, it all started with Dubai's daring inspiration to create a city of grand *imagery* and opulence that would attract the world's elite to their new playground of real estate, new technology, excellence, and human enterprise. When I first began to view the plans of development—which were advertised in special newspaper sections—to create numerous man-made islands, to be filled with hotels, beaches, fitness centers, spas, water parks, restaurants, resorts, shopping malls, townhouses, business centers, and international hubs for trade and entertainment, I considered the idea to be unbelievable. Its leaders and business investors actually planned to create new land—from which to build elaborate centers of work, life, and play—using sand dredged from the nearby sea water.

When you talk about grand scale branding and *imagery*, the city of Dubai obviously took the term seriously. I wanted to see these man-made islands and coming attractions immediately! The city's goal now is to become a leading territory of human imagination and enterprise in the world. With the planned development and construction of multiple projects still ongoing-as the brainchild and design of Sheikh Mohammed bin Rashid Al Maktoum, the ruler of Dubai—the city plans to attract 15 million visitors by year 2010, and increase its population to 3 million by 2017. Government officials and business promoters have already began to solicit the world's elite for a number of investment and entertainment packages that will continue to propel Dubai's growing and prosperous economy.

Understanding the power of *imagery* has helped to enhance successful business brands of not only Cadillac and the city of Dubai, but of other corporations and prosperous industries around the world. However, like the other 19 elements of this text, creating and utilizing a personal or company brand takes effort. Whether we believe it makes a difference or not, people are always watching. Sometimes new businesses are able to slip in under the radar and surprise the masses with unique goals and services. However, as soon as your specific *imagery* becomes publicized and familiar, the element of surprise disappears. You will then be forced to work hard to maintain your good company name, or reinvent yourself if needed. But if you desire to reach the next level of *support*, you will learn to either *use* your *imagery*, or you will *lose* it. So give the public something to identify with and to buy into.

Like the McDonald's arch, the Nike Swoosh, the three stripes of Adidas, the Polo man, the MGM lion, the Warner Brothers W, the red Target bull's-eye, the Izod alligator, the Kangol kangaroo, and hundreds of other recognizable names and brands, the Cadillac shield and reef continues to signify a specific goal, design, and product of business. Likewise, the nation of Dubai has begun to promote its own brand within the international business and tourism industry.

But for those of you who are not comfortable with the idea of putting yourself or your company out in the public eye for branding, allow me to make another note about *imagery*. When the momentum of popularity and recognition is apparent, and you can sense the *support* growing behind you, take this as your chance to ride the wave. If you back down, you may miss the opportunity you need for favorable public exposure, and will have no one to blame but yourself. So you either create a workable image for the masses to admire, follow and aspire to, or you may find your goals, products, and services left behind and forgotten.

The bottom line with *imagery* is this: major companies, corporations, multimedia empires, successful entertainers, entrepreneurs, athletes, cities, states, nations, and serious brand makers have all been able to reach, influence, and become familiar to millions of people around the world through quality products, services, and recognizable *imagery*. It takes the extra effort in order to make a business expand faster, and to maintain the imagination and *support* of an audience. Now ask yourself honestly—what range of people have you actively influenced with your personal or company image?

The Imagery Chart
Please Consider Your Most Honest Mark Below

Communal—Local—Regional—National—World

Imagery may not seal the deal by itself; but if people recognize and are excited by the ideas that you or your company represent, that excitement and recognition will surely make transactions easier. So learn to do whatever is needed to create and maintain a workable public image for your personal and company brand and goals. And it's never too late introduce one.

In the last section, "The Equation in Use," you may continue to fill in your chart.

MOVEMENT

At this point in the text, we have reached the bridge of *The Equation*. The goal now is to attract the supporters who will help propel us across that bridge and into the Purple Section of success, *progress*, and wealth. With a show of *support* in the forms of capital, the inclusion of skills, votes of confidence, background assistance, present attendance, moral defense, endorsements, and shared experience, we will be able to reach our goals. Crossing this bridge toward actualized *business* is the same process for all successful individuals and companies. It must happen! And it comes to pass through the most important element called *movement*.

Webster's Third New International Dictionary defines the word *movement* as the action or process of moving; change of place or position or posture. *Movement* is also a particular impulse or inclination; a progression in a particular direction or toward a particular objective. Finally, a *movement* is a series of actions taken by a body of persons to achieve such objective.

We must all understand that *talking* about success alone will not make it happen. *Planning* for success does not make it happen. Being *prepared* for success will not make it happen. Having the *potential* for success will not make it happen. Success is only achieved through *movement*—*movement* from proactive individuals and companies who seek successful business, as well as *movement* from a reactive population who are willing to *support* us in our goals. But if there is no *pro*-activity from a business source, and no *re*-activity from a targeted or influenced audience, there will *be* no business.

Business does not create itself. Forces of *movement* create business. So if you have no *movement*, you have no business—plain and simple.

The business *movement* of a healthier fast-food choice was launched in 1999, after the 240-pound weight loss of a now-famous undergrad from Indiana University, Jared Fogle. Subsisting on a diet of Subway sandwiches for lunch and dinner, and buffered by the consistent exercise of walking, Fogle dropped from more than 400 pounds to under 200 in a matter of months.

When a former roommate, Ryan Coleman, published an article about Fogle's miraculous weight loss on a Subway sandwich diet in the *Indiana Daily Student*, a reporter for *Men's Health* saw the article and included the Subway Sandwich Diet in an article on "Crazy Diets That Work." The article then caught the eye of a Chicago-area Subway franchise owner Bob Ocwieja, who brought the story to the attention of Richard Coad, the creative director at Subway's Chicago advertising agency.

As the *movement* of the story continued, Coad and his boss, Barry Krause, sent an intern to Bloomington, Indiana, to track down the "Subway guy." Asking around at a Subway franchise near Indiana University's campus, the intern struck gold and was able to confirm Jared Fogle's story.

Coad and Ocwieja took the idea to Subway's new marketing director with hopes of turning the student's amazing testimony into an ad campaign. But the duo were rebuked, and told that such "healthy fast food" diets had been unsuccessfully attempted in the past and might even create a legal liability for the company. The advertising director responded that a medical turnaround as severe as Jared Fogle's could not be attributed to eating sandwiches.

Nevertheless, Coad and his boss Krause decided to try a regional ad campaign—an idea that was championed by owners of local Subway franchises in the area. Incredibly, Krause was so moved by Fogle's story, that he decided to go out on a limb to shoot and finance the regional commercial—which would not be funded by the Subway company.

Airing on January 1, 2000, and introducing Jared Fogle and his story with a disclaimer, the regional commercial became a stunning success, and produced phone calls from *USA Today*, ABC News, Fox News, and the *Oprah Winfrey Show*. Barry Krause was then called by Subway's national advertising director to ask if the spot could be aired nationally.

As a result of Jared Fogle's overwhelming appeal, Subway's year 2000 sales exceeded those of the previous year by 18 percent. In 2001, the sales figures rose another 16 percent, as Jared Fogle became a national phenomenon and a Subway company pitch man. Since Fogle's advertising campaign began, with more than 50 separate commercials, the Subway company sales have more than doubled to an $8.2 billion industry in 2008. In fact, Fogle's positive *movement* of Subway customers has been so overwhelming that a brief departure from his ads in year 2005, coincided with a 10 percent drop in company sales, compelling the company to bring them back.

Now that's *movement!* Every part of Jared Fogle's story represents a perfect case study of the *proactive* and *reactive* forces that are needed to produce a successful business. At any break in the long chain of these events—starting with Jared's decision to maintain a Subway sandwich diet that included constant walking, down to the advertising representatives who started the ad campaign without payment, to the franchise owners who agreed to *support* it, the media professionals who continued to run with the story, and the general public who eventually became inspired to buy millions more of Subway sandwiches—none of this tremendous business would have happened.

The Subway company, started in 1965 by Fred DeLuca and Dr. Peter Buck in Bridgeport, Connecticut—although not hurting for business prior to Jared Fogle's campaign—benefited from his popularity with leaps and bounds. Recently named the #1 Global

Franchise Opportunity by *Entrepreneur Magazine*, the Subway franchise is the largest restaurant chain in North America, and is poised to become the largest restaurant chain in the world, with over 22,000 locations in 78 countries.

In addition to featuring a variety of low-fat menu options, Subway offers an equally appetizing display of healthful side items, from sliced apples; yogurt, milk, and raisins. Not only has Subway joined the healthy fast-food *movement*, the sandwich company has joined the go-green *movement* as well, opening their first eco-friendly store in November of 2007, with plans to open several more eco-friendly stores in the future.

Another tremendous example of a full-speed-ahead business *movement*, was the explosive relevance of the Cable News Network (CNN) during the first Persian Gulf War of 1991. CNN, initially founded by multimedia mogul Ted Turner in 1980, was established as the first network to provide 24-hour television news coverage. Utilizing a general crew of low-paid reporters, the CNN station was no match for the big three networks: ABC, NBC, and CBS news. But exclusive and continuous CNN coverage of the first Persian Gulf War-with historical live reports from the al-Rashid Hotel in Baghdad-catapulted Turner's Cable News Network past the big three in ratings for the first time in its history. On a monumental scoop, CNN was the only news outlet with the ability to communicate outside of Iraq during the initial hours of the American bombing campaign.

The Gulf War experience brought CNN much sought-after legitimacy and made household names of its previously unknown reporters, including Bernard Shaw, John Holliman, Peter Arnett, Pentagon correspondent Wolf Blitzer, and international correspondent Christiane Amanpour. They quickly became the new gold standard in breaking international news.

The up close and personal CNN coverage of the war sent the network's stock value skyrocketing and made Ted Turner a bona fide mogul. His upstart network would become the new national leader in cable network news coverage, with headquarters at the CNN Center in Atlanta, the Time Warner Center in New York, and studios in Washington, DC. With a 24-hour news advantage, and recognition, CNN was also the first network to break news on the September 11, 2001, attacks on New York's World Trade Center, in reports anchored by Carol Lin.

To date, the network is available in 93 million American households, with 10 domestic bureaus and more than 900 affiliated local stations. The news network is also available in nearly a million hotel rooms. Globally, CNN airs through CNN International with 26 international bureaus and network services that are available to more than 1.5 billion people in over 212 countries and territories. Rated as America's number one cable news source, and ranked number two behind the Fox News in total audience, CNN is also number two internationally, behind the much older British Broadcast Channel(BBC).

Despite international criticisms that the network has a pro-American perspective, as well as domestic criticism that it is too liberal or anti-American, CNN has become a reliable international news force with multiple spinoffs, including Headline News, CNN.com, CNN Pipeline, CNN en Espanol, and various others. With a line up of highly-viewed news talk shows, reports, and recognizable media brands, including *CNN Newsroom, Larry King Live, Anderson Cooper 360, Late Edition with Wolf Blitzer, Reliable Sources* hosted by *Washington Post* media critic Howard Kurtz, and *Your $$$$$* hosted by Ali Veshi and Christine Romans, CNN has solidified its business and news value for years to come.

Like the expansion, marketing, and promotion of Subway fast-food restaurants, the international relevance of CNN, highlight the very important element of business *movement* at work. As in their examples, *movement* is often effective at closing in on a customer base through constant information and access. We then eventually buy into successful businesses because they often surround us at every turn with *attractive* branding, *packaging*, and competitive pricing. We buy Subway sandwiches because their *organization* has succeeded at pushing a healthier food choice while placing chain stores in areas that are easy to find. We watch CNN because the network's importance and *imagery* in breaking international news is now fully recognizable. And in general, we *support* most businesses because we are *used* to them. Through our familiarity, these successful businesses are able to create consistent *movement* whether we claim to personally like them or not.

So what do the other fast food restaurants or television networks do to compete? They create proactive and reactive *counter-movement* with *attraction, packaging, organization,* and *imagery* of their own.

Big business events of *movement* are designed to make us respond accordingly. Effective business methods are calculated to gain the strongest *support* by surrounding us with successful elements of strategy. And at the end of the day, *movement* is our goal. We want a body of supporters to *love* our value, our products, and our services with *passion, commitment, dedication, loyalty,* and *consistency.* We want our particular skills of *art* to create *adoration, presentation, purpose, execution,* and *excellence.* And the end result is our desire to build *support* that is acquired through *attraction, packaging, organization,* and *imagery* that establishes *movement* from those groups of supporters that we hope to inspire, enlighten, or excite with our goods.

Now ask yourself honestly—by using your own elements of *attraction, packaging, organization,* and *imagery,* what range of people have you been able to *move* to *support* your personal or company products and services? And I am definitely referring to *real* numbers here—quantities that tell you about sales, votes, time, company stock, lessons, staff, attendance—anything concrete to validate real *movement* from the public toward your objectives. Once you are able to assess all of the honest numbers, you will then know what you need to work on.

The Movement Chart
Please Consider Your Most Honest Mark Below

Communal — Local — Regional — National — World

In the final section, "The Equation in Use," you may now average your totals of *support* to devise your Representation of Support Number, or RSN.

BUSINESS IS ROYALTY

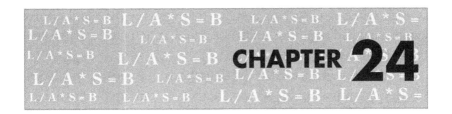

CHAPTER 24

THE DEFINITION
OF BUSINESS

We have now successfully crossed the bridge of three indisputable components and fifteen elements to reach the right side of *The Equation*. Here we deal with the stand-alone component of *business*—or what I refer to as "royalty." In this new day and age, royalty is defined less by the lineage of kings and queens and more defined by the individuals, partners, and companies of successful enterprises. Successful *business* is the *new* royalty, as represented by the color purple. And within this Purple Section, symbolized by a *wine glass*—as an image of wealth, value, and leisure—we will discuss the final Five Elements that allow us all to determine our Business Equivalent Number, or BEN.

Webster's Third New International Dictionary defines *business* as purposeful activity; activity directed toward an immediate and specific end; activity engaged or extended over a period of time; commercial or mercantile activity; activity engaged in as a means to livelihood; or activity typically involving some independence. *Business* is also defined as judgment of power of decision; a commercial or industrial enterprise; a place where such an enterprise is carried on; transactions of any nature; the procedures or techniques of such enterprise; serious activity that requires time and effort; avoidance of distracting influences; and activity of a particular field or endeavor.

The common theme for the definitions of *business* is the use of strong, definitive action words: "activity," "directed," "engaged," "extended," "livelihood," "involving," "independence," "judgment," "power," "decision," "commercial," "industrial," "enterprise," "transactions," "procedures," "techniques," "serious," "effort," "avoiding distraction."

We can also include the simple root word of *business*, which is to be *busy*. In the Red Section, we asked ourselves the question, "How *warm* are we toward our career goals?" In the Gold Section, we asked, "How *good* are we at our particular skills?" In the Green Section, we asked, "How many *people* can we *move* in the direction of our objectives?" And now that we've arrived at the Purple Section, we must ask ourselves the final questions: "How *busy* are we in our quest toward continued progress?" and "How *successful* have we been at achieving our goals?"

Like the definitive action words that define it, *business* is about activity—*always!* The simple question posed in many everyday phone calls from one person to another is "Are you busy?" In other words, "Are you presently engaged in the daily activity that will create the achievement of your goals?"

Most *business* people assume that you are just as busy as they are. For an entrepreneur or a company, the activity of enterprise is as normal as breathing. So agreed-upon times and meeting places are scheduled to create opportunities for two or more entities to interact. Nevertheless, in order for these *business* meetings to be useful for either party, agree-upon transactions must be executed toward their benefit. And if a thousand daily meetings between *business* parties do not produce successful transactions, then the ultimate goal of *business* has not been achieved.

In Mexico, 68-year-old Carlos Slim—an entrepreneur with controlling ownership of more than 200 companies—has been successful in *business* transactions over and over again. Slim, a one-time math instructor with an engineering degree from

Universidad Nacional Autonoma de Mexico, learned his knack for numbers through his father Julian Slim—a Lebanese immigrant. Julian—who established new enterprises and bought real estate in downtown Mexico during the 1910 Revolution—required his young son Carlos to record his childhood purchases in note-books. By the time young Carlos had matured into an adult, he had become well schooled on how to create, invest, and engage in money-making enterprises.

In the early 1960s, Slim—a recent college graduate—started a stock brokerage in Mexico City and began to acquire industrial companies he deemed to be bargains. He would then reinvest his gains in the existing businesses or use the cash to acquire additional properties, naming the holding company Grupo Carso.

When the Mexican economy crashed in 1982—with the country defaulting on foreign-debt payments—investors fled the country and stopped their interests in Mexican industry, allowing Slim to scoop up various company stock and assets at bargain basement prices. By the late 1980s—when the Mexican economy began to recover—Carlos Slim had become one of the country's most successful businessmen.

Slim then developed successful partnerships with the South-western Bell Company (SBC) and France Telecom to seize a percentage ownership of the state-owned telephone company, Telefonos de Mexico (TelMex) in 1990, after the Mexican government put the telephone company up for sale to spark privatization of national enterprises. The idea was the creation of Carlos Salinas, a Harvard-educated government official bent on modernizing the country. Salinas referred to Slim as one of the brightest young businessmen in Mexico, and the two developed a friendship.

Taking advantage of his skills in company takeovers, as well as his friendships in *business*, Slim benefited from a seven-year guarantee for TelMex to remain the only telephone company in Mexico, which secured his success in providing the nation's dominant phone service. He then solidified his hold in the telephone industry by cornering the market on the copper cables used by Telmex for telephone wires and went on to invest in Mexican cell phone service, Internet communications, restaurants, cigarettes, construction, mining, bicycles, soft drinks, airlines, hotels, railways, banking, printing, and more recently community development.

To make certain his *business* enterprises would continue to progress, Slim trained his three sons—Carlos Jr., Marco Antonio, and Patrick—from an early age to successfully manage his various companies, as well as to recognize, create, and invest in new enterprises of their own. Increasing his net worth to more than $60 billion, Carlos Slim's only rivals on the Forbes 400 list are Bill Gates and Warren Buffett. Like the legendary John D. Rockefeller, Slim has invested in the control of so many Mexican enterprises that his holdings are worth a third of the nation's stock exchange. There are few *business* transactions in Mexico that he does not personally gain from.

Some *business* moguls call it being in the right place at the right time. Some call it luck. And others call it good business sense. But critics tend to call them old-fashioned monopolies. Regardless of what we may all personally believe about the success of big enterprises, the first lesson of progressive *business* remains the same: to acquire vehicles that make more revenue than they lose, and to deposit more money than you withdraw.

Creating, mastering, organizing, promoting, and investing in successful *business* opportunities and enterprises are the goals of every successful individual and company in this book—no matter *how* they do it. But to *remain* successful in your *business* endeavors, you must eventually become efficient at recognizing the bottom line of a winning balance sheet. Individuals and companies who thrive in deciding who, what, when, where, why and how much to invest their time, effort, and capital—concerning services, products, and industries—will be capable of producing and maintaining more continuous *business* than those who do not.

As the example of Carlos Slim depicts, progressive enterprise is all about knowing your numbers, and using every advantage and skill possible to secure success. Whether your strength is in the red energy of *passion*, the gold skills of *art*, or the green cultivation of *movement*, the ultimate goal is to create the purple wealth and endurance of a successful *business*.

Like many moguls and corporations around the world-by studying all of the details, knowing what to invest in, and outdoing the competition—Mr. Slim continues to gain and is rumored to have rarely taken a loss. For many successful entrepreneurs around the globe, winning big has become the normal expectation of *business*. But the key is to win—*period*—at any level. All successful entrepreneurs and companies start with their first buy and sell of a service or product—including you.

Therefore, the *business* symbol of a half-filled *wine glass* is all up to the beholder. How much wine do *you* pour? How *expensive* is your wine? How many partners and or associates do you intend to share your wine *with*? And how expensive are your *wine glasses*?

To be considered successful in *business*, one must have the ability to enjoy the spoils of one's hard-earned work and wealth and to *add* to it. You must have the ability to buy and enjoy enough wine to pour at your *leisure*—which means that your hard work has already paid off handsome dividends. But if it has not, and you are not able to enjoy your wealth without even more legwork, then you have not yet crossed the bridge of *The Equation* successfully, and your goal of *business* is still a work in *progress*.

CHAPTER 25

WHY THE COLOR PURPLE?

Historically, the color purple has represented royalty, and was the color worn by members of the royal guard. Purple is a combination color that is created from a mix of red and blue—which would symbolize *business* as a blueprint or a design for action. This red-blue creation of dye was mass produced, tailored, and worn to mark individuals who lived at the higher levels of social hierarchies. For thousands of years, the symbolic relationship between the color purple and the *imagery* of royalty has persisted.

The perception of royalty and its symbolic color of purple has also been long associated with lineage—or wealth that is passed down through generations. However, in a present-day society of competitive enterprise, driven individuals—including those from adverse circumstances of poverty—have risen to become wealthy, respected, and powerful icons, who inspire millions and become royal in their own right. Such is the case of billionaire, multimedia icon Oprah Winfrey.

Like many other entrepreneurs of successful *business*, Oprah has risen to first-generation wealth, and has become one of the most influential women in the world. Through determination, independence, hard work, belief, and overwhelming ambition, she has produced consistent success in many media for more than 30 years.

With a reputation among family, friends, and instructors as a hard-working, fast-reading, Bible-quoting, contest-winning, honor student—who was always involved in something noteworthy—Oprah began her career at the age of 17 at a local radio station, while attending Tennessee State University. Born and raised in Mississippi, she became the most popular girl wherever she moved—from Milwaukee, Wisconsin, to the suburb of Glendale, and back down to Nashville, Tennessee, where she won the Miss Black Tennessee beauty pageant at 18. She then became the state's youngest anchor and the first black woman at Nashville's WLAC-TV.

She later moved to Baltimore, where she co-anchored the six o'clock news at WJZ-TV in 1976, before being recruited to join the network's *People Are Talking* show as the co-host—a job that included a stint as the host of a local Baltimore version of *Dialing for Dollars*.

After being fired from the network in Baltimore, and told that she was not quite what television viewers wanted, Oprah relocated to Chicago for history-making success—or should we say, "her-story"-making?

In the Windy City, Oprah Winfrey would eventually host an initially low-rated, half-hour talk show called *AM Chicago* on WLS-TV. Her first episode aired on January 2, 1984—and she managed to move the show's ratings from last to first in a year. She was simultaneously able to overtake the nationally known Phil Donahue as the highest rated talk show in Chicago. WLS-TV then decided to rename the program the *Oprah Winfrey Show* and expanded the time to a full hour. In September of 1986, the show was broadcast nationally.

The *Oprah Winfrey Show* went head to head with *Donahue* on a national platform, and Oprah soon passed Phil's number one spot—a status achievement that made her the leading daytime talk show host in America.

During the mid 1980s, at the same time that her syndicated talk show was beginning to garner national acclaim, Oprah co-starred in a feature film production of Alice Walker's best-selling novel—ironically titled *The Color Purple*.

As Sophia, Oprah Winfrey was cast as a proud, fearless, and embattled African-American woman, who inspires courage in her oppressed peers. Her strong portrayal of a free, broken, and then rejuvenated woman led to an Academy Award nomination for Best Supporting Actress. Her successful film role helped to increase the *Oprah Winfrey Show's* national ratings even more.

But Oprah was far from finished. Changing the platform of her show to one of spiritual uplift, she began to land the biggest celebrity interviews on television—interviews that included once in a life time confessions that topped Barber Walters' evening dialogue. Oprah then secured a steadily increasing points deal—with the help of attorney Jeff Jacobs–by making King World Productions the show's national distributor. The deal quickly landed Oprah in the multimillionaire range; and it continues to increase her wealth.

Forming her own company—which she named Harpo Productions—Oprah went on to produce feature films, a national book club, and host various big events. She launched the television careers of friends, produced successful magazines, online media, bought national real estate, landed a multi-million-dollar satellite radio deal, and secured a deal to run her own television network. The list grows longer to this day, as millions of Oprah's loyal supporters proceed to back her in her many efforts.

While maintaining her ties to the African-American community, Oprah went on to command an incredibly supportive audience of mainstream, white American women—who would make her the dominant voice and vehicle for the consumer power of Baby Boomer housewives born in the 1950s—a phenomenal audience of millions.

Like other Purple business people and royal figures of history, Oprah became a generous contributor to many national causes and charities. She has donated millions of her own wealth and raised millions more through her Oprah's Angels Network to benefit those in need, for a total of more than $300 million—including more than $20 million to the states of Louisiana, Alabama, Mississippi, and Texas after the tragedies of Hurricanes Katrina and Rita.

In South Africa, Oprah invested $40 million and much of her personal time, *dedication*, and effort, to establish the Oprah Winfrey Leadership Academy for Girls near Johannesburg, where she became the queen mother of hundreds of disadvantaged youth.

She has also used her purple *business* power and worldwide influence to broaden awareness and acceptance of the artistic value, *passion*, and *excellence* of many other African-American women of stature.

As the queen of all media, Oprah continues to be active, directed, engaged, extended, lively, involved, independent, powerful, decisive, commercial, industrial, and enterprising with every aspect of her *business*—including transactions, procedures, and techniques that have been consistently successful. She has also avoided pitfalls and distractions that would hinder her steady rise and *movement* toward progress.

Oprah Winfrey Inc. is by all means a royal *business* of Purple stature; and she has spent more than a dozen years on the Forbes 400 list as the longest-reigning self-made woman and African-American. Her present net worth has been estimated at more than $2.5 billion and counting, where she holds court as one of the world's most dominant business women.

Now that's what it means to be *purple*—to acquire notable *income, productivity, progress, power* and *responsibility*—with plenty of wealth and leisure to enjoy a glass of wine. These are The Five Elements of *business*. And all around the world—in the twenty-first century—big *business* has become synonymous with royalty. Royalty has been historically represented by the color purple, and now so is *business*.

INCOME

Webster's Third New International Dictionary defines the word *income*—as it relates to the field of *business*—as a gain or recurrent benefit that is usually measured in money and for the given period of time, derives from capital, labor, or a combination of both, includes gains from transactions in capital assets, but excludes unrealized advances in value. *Income* is also commercial revenue or receipts of any kind except receipts or returns of capital. Finally, *income* is the value of goods and services received by an individual in a given period of time.

Okay . . . the gloves are now off. It's time to break down and rebuild egos—a necessary evil to understanding the harsh realities of the *business* world. This chapter on *income* is where we establish the truth of the many economic layers of society. The fact is that not everyone will become entrepreneurs or purple *business* people. However, in a free society, we are all able at least to *pursue* the needed opportunities to achieve *business execution* and ownership, as well as to provide economic growth and security for ourselves, for our families, and for our employees. A sufficient *income* will allow us to carry out those goals.

The first question you must answer concerning the evaluation of *income* is "What *is* my *business?*" Whether you work for yourself, for someone else, for a partnership, or within the rank and file of a large company, you must be able to answer the basic question: "What product or service do I provide?"

Once you are able to answer that question, you must quantify how much that product or service is worth. In other words, how much does your product of service cost? If you are not in a position directly related to sales, you must still be able to justify the expense of your position. What is the value of the contribution your personal *art* brings to your company? And is your contribution specialized enough to call your position an *art*, or are you just a generic employee?

As we have now crossed the bridge from the Green Section to the Purple Section, we find that the *business* component of *The Equation* is extremely significant, as well as unapologetic. It is in the Purple Section where millions of dollars are gained and lost every hour. At this level, the numbers are the facts, and there is little tolerance for underperformance. So when a purple executive asks what you are worth or what you would like to be paid, your honest answer should correspond to the value of the *love, art,* and *support* that you bring to your company.

All the components and elements of *The Equation* sum up to this: If you don't have enough *love* for the field of work you are in to effectively demonstrate it or your skills are not developed enough to be considered an *art* and you therefore lack the *support* to back your endeavors, then you will be forced to accept whatever *income* a *business* executive may offer you.

Let me make this statement perfectly clear: Individuals who live within the realm of the Purple Section are *not* in the *business* of investing in any person, company, or product without expecting a return. Even when *business* interactions involve charity, there is the value of a taxable write-off or a personal *passion* to help a certain cause or group of people that a purple person believes in. But if a purple person does not believe in you—and your *love, art,* or *support* is not strong enough to convince them—you will be rendered powerless, unless you are able to create your own *power*—which will land you back at the initial chapter of *The Equation*.

Understanding the importance of *income*, entrepreneurship, and goal-oriented employment are essential tools to succeed in *business*. Running our own enterprises—from start to finish—provides us with opportunities to gain experience while strengthening personal skills. Entrepreneurship also teaches us all about the necessity of working capital.

However, without short- and long-term goals of improving yourself and your organization or endeavor, starting an enterprise or accepting any position that produces *income* will leave you at the mercy of the basic laws of capitalism, where assets (or *income* gains) are always threatened by liabilities (or *income* losses). And if you or your enterprise is perceived as an *income* loss, few companies or individuals will hire or invest in you.

Would you knowingly hire or invest in a person or product that you expect to lose money on—with no expectation of a gain? Successful *business* people *will* not and *do* not. And when they do make mistakes with employees or investments, they eventually correct them with firings, company sales, and liquidations.

However, the effective management of *income* allows you, as an individual or company, to become the boss of your own investments. So if you are fortunate enough to establish an independent *income* source, then do so. Or continue to make yourself an asset to the company you work for while always striving to improve personal *productivity* for the next opportunity that comes your way. If you are driven enough to trust your own *business* instincts—with the competent use of *income*—you become *purple* yourself.

All the individual or company case studies that have been highlighted in this book, as well as thousands of other successful individuals and companies, have utilized their *income* gains to expand their objectives in *business* and to increase their productive turnover. Reinvestment in your enterprise is the surest way to control your own economic destiny. And those who have done so successfully, have gained tremendously.

Take, for example, the *income* reinvestment of Earvin "Magic" Johnson, the superstar Los Angeles Lakers' point guard from the legendary 1980s showtime teams. Instead of blowing all of his wealth and settling into old age and a rocking chair, in the early 1990s Magic Johnson immediately turned to entrepreneurship and a failed television talk show experiment called *The Magic Hour*. Undeterred and restless, Johnson remained energized and optimistic about jump starting a new career, and he was convinced that urban communities held a tremendous amount of consumer power that was still untapped.

Realizing that he still had a recognizable and attractive brand name after basketball—with plenty of community *support*— Johnson set out to establish economic development in urban areas with use of his own *income*, resources, and personal relationships.

Forming Magic Johnson Enterprises with an immediate *purpose*, Johnson began to make persistent phone calls to the *purple business* people who had become friends with throughout his basketball career. His plans were to have them invest in the revitalization of African-American communities through viable partnership opportunities.

African-Americans attended theaters and enjoyed feature films, but they often had to leave their own areas to *support* suburban or other outside community establishments. So Magic Johnson called and spoke to Travis Reid, the purple CEO of Loews Cineplex Entertainment, about a movie theater deal next to the Baldwin Hills Mall in Inglewood, California, near L.A. The partnership led to the first Magic Johnson Theater, featuring multiple screens. Loews then partnered to open Magic Johnson theaters across the country, including theaters in Atlanta, Georgia, and Harlem.

Johnson made a similar call to Howard Schultz, the purple CEO of Starbuck's Coffee, to convince him that African-Americans would buy and drink coffee in L.A.—like everyone else. A few extra phone calls were needed before Schultz took Magic seriously, but when he finally took heed of his persistence, their flagship franchise in Inglewood had a tremendous first year, leading to a Magic Johnson Starbuck's Coffee partnership that would open more than 100 new franchises in 14 states.

Johnson struck another partnership with the T.G.I. Friday's restaurant chain, and has established urban American real estate and development through a Canyon Capital fund. He established the Magic Johnson Foundation for urban charity, developed business management programs, advocated for small business loans, and promoted national health initiatives for HIV awareness. He also established the Magic Johnson Entertainment arm—with music and film projects—all of which provided opportunities, development, housing, and *income* for hundreds of African-American employees, managers, and entrepreneurs across the country.

More recently, Magic Johnson Enterprises partnered with the Burger King corporation, opening dozens of new Burger King franchises in the southeastern United States to create opportunity and *income* for hundreds more in underdeveloped urban areas. He secured a *business* relationship with the fruit and soft drink brand of Cranbury, a partnership with Caribbean travel cruise lines, agreed to an urban marketing deal with Best Buy electronics, and has established a chain of 24-hour fitness health spas.

Presently estimated at a net worth of $700 million, the economic empire of former athlete Magic Johnson continues to grow. In April 2008 the Canyon-Johnson Urban Fund for real estate development drew its largest investment yet—$1 billion from pension funds and other investors. But this would not have been possible without Johnson's past, present, and ongoing command of *income*. Purple investors first had to learn to respect him as a legitimate businessman and not just as an athlete. But now they've witnessed his Magic Johnson Enterprises turn into an urban development powerhouse.

Johnson is just one example out of many entrepreneurs who was ready and willing to put his own money where his mouth was, while challenging others to join him. And where plenty of athletes, entertainers, and celebrity talents are able to command multimillion-dollar contracts and agreements during the height of their careers, the understanding of their *income* and brand name popularity would allow more of them to create new *business* opportunities for themselves, for their families, and for their communities after their careers begin to wane.

Magic Johnson now appears at many national and community events to speak about economic opportunity and empowerment in the African-American and urban communities. He has also invested in a percentage of the purple and gold Los Angeles Lakers basketball franchise with his old boss, Jerry Buss, securing yet another opportunity of future *business*. And he has received various community and corporate business awards for his active outreach and service.

Even if some of us will never reach Magic Johnson's level of fame or fortune, the understanding of *income* is useful not only for those who can command large performance contracts, but also for every individual with a paycheck and a desire to control her own destiny. You alone determine how you spend your own money, and no one else. Even small amounts of *income* invested in a new enterprise are often enough to get started in the direction of economic independence.

I began the journey of my own purple status as a writer, entrepreneur, and publisher with a $500 paycheck, and contributions and loans from family members and friends. As soon as I made enough *income* to print, distribute, and market my own books without the need of investors, I continued to reinvest my earnings to grow my *business*. Economic liberty is what reinvested *income* provides to any *business*.

For all of us, the key to the utilization of *income* is to educate ourselves on how best to maximize the capital and opportunities that we have, which includes reinvesting in the company you work for, finding your own small investments on the side, forming partnerships with positive *income* start-ups, buying affordable real estate, or investing in 401(k) plans. If no bank, family member, friend, or private investor will back you on your plans to diversify, be courageous enough to invest in yourself through thrift and savings. But by all means, make sure that your investment *works* and creates more *income*.

It may sound frivolous to those of you who still don't understand the score, but respect for *income* is a royal game. Purple people respect hard cash—period. Hard cash and *income* is what made them purple in the first place. So if you lack the necessary *income, business* hustle, or decision-making skills to earn the royal color, you may be pushed back across the bridge to green—where you'll find yourself at the mercy of purple people again, and you'll have to work all the harder to prove that you deserve a bigger check.

This chapter on *income* asks you to evaluate your personal and *company* value for a *purpose.* The *purpose* is to inspire serious thought about the *movement* of *income*—no matter how small. If you are able to learn how *income* works—how to earn it, how to keep it, how to multiply it, how to move it around, and how to invest it—the purple people will learn to respect you; they will invest in your projects, and they will invite you to join them at the country golf clubs and at the negotiation tables. Once you become a purple person yourself—and become friends and associates of royalty—you'll be amazed at how many of the bigger deals fall right into your lap without nearly as much effort. I have personally been there and done that—so I know how it all works.

In the final section, "The Equation in Use," you may now take your BEN, or Business Equivalent Number, divide it into your actual *income*—which corresponds to that particular year of your Equation Chart—and multiply it by 100 percent to find: Your Value of Income.

I explain this number in more detail in "The Equation in Use."

PRODUCTIVITY

Webster's Third New International Dictionary defines the word *productivity* as an abundance of richness in output; the physical output per unit of productive effort. *Productivity* is also referred to as the degree of effectiveness of industrial management in utilizing the facilities for production; the effectiveness in utilizing labor and equipment.

If you have never heard the statement before that "product is king," I'll explain it to you another way: Without *productivity* there is no *business*. Every *business* around the world involves selling, buying, advertising, promoting, trading, financing, analyzing, watching, enjoying, critiquing, listening to, investing in, using, eating, cooking, decorating, reading, creating, building, destroying, repairing, driving, flying, navigating, shipping, receiving, preparing, testing, washing, cleaning, storing, shelving, collecting, modeling, and displaying . . . *goods*. And without goods, we have nothing left to talk about. That's how important *productivity* is. Whoever are the first, the most efficient, consistent, adored, or cost-effective at creating, producing, promoting, distributing, and selling goods, products, and services will become the purple people.

Productivity is the driving force behind every enterprise. We must continue to produce goods and services in order to create

155

sales and profits. So as the famous Dunkin' Donuts commercial states—no matter what—*productivity* demands that it's "Time to make the donuts."

Featuring "Fred the Baker" as a sleepy-eyed manager of a Dunkin' Donuts franchise, who makes early-morning trips to the store to bake fresh donuts for his customers, the 1980s commercial won honors from the Television Bureau of Advertising as one of the five best commercials of its era. The campaign also produced a golden catchphrase promoting *productivity*. Whether your product or service is donuts, noodles, hamburgers, T-shirts, shoes, automobile maintenance, landscaping, fingernail repairs, plumbing, or trash collection, in order to remain in business your *productivity* must grow.

Not only did Dunkin' Donuts produce the obvious varieties of fresh-baked donuts and pastries, the successful franchise also sells bagels, muffins, cookies, coffee, breakfast croissants, hash browns, hot chocolate, tea, fruit smoothies, and cold beverages, and has recently added pizza and flatbread sandwiches to its menu.

Founded by William Rosenberg in 1950 as a simple donut and coffee shop in Quincy, Massachusetts, the Dunkin' Donuts franchise spread across the northeast and beyond to include 36 states, before expanding globally for a total of more than 7,000 stores, serving 2.7 million customers per day. That equates to a whole lot of donuts. And the product has remained basically the same: jellies, creams, glazed, fruit filled, sprinkled, and sugared donuts.

While positioning the franchise as a one-stop shop for all things breakfast—and now including lunch and dinner items—Dunkin' Donuts has remained competitive with Starbucks and Krispy Kreme by featuring coffee at much more reasonable prices than Starbucks, and offering more varieties of donuts and foods than Krispy Kreme. And with steady *productivity*, Dunkin' Donuts has continued in its success and popularity to the tune of $4.7 billion a year.

"Time to make the donuts" is right. *Business* must remain busy. But what about when *productivity* is slowed to a halt—due to disagreements between the production staff and the corporation? What happens then? Take, for example, the recent Hollywood writers strike. Many common citizens were not informed about the details. But to make it easy to understand—every time we create new technology to utilize old intellectual properties—like films, television shows, music, and books—the major multimedia companies who secure the rights to produce the properties are able to make new money from them. So as we go out and update our old VHS tapes to DVDs, and then our old DVDs to Blu-Ray discs, and our Blu-Ray discs to something else in five years, money is made from an old product. That's a great form of *productivity* and a major reason why multimedia brands love to own time-less material that people will always want to watch, read, or listen to.

Instead of having to create an entirely new product, companies pay to upgrade existing properties into new formats, repackage them for promotion, and then resell the properties to a community that already loves the product.

However, that old product has original creators who have royalties due. So if, for example, a publishing company creates an Internet book based on an author's old material, the publisher is aware that the author is still owed his or her share of royalty percentages based on the new format. Therefore, this author will receive updated addendums—or legal additions to their existing contracts—every time a new technology comes out that publishers may use to execute new product sales.

What prompted the writers' strike was when television networks began to make deals on Internet technology—through which old television shows could be watched online—without cutting in a writer's percentage on the deal. And—rightfully—all hell broke loose. The Writers Guild understood that if they did not make a move to protect the intellectual property rights and royalties due to their creative writers—in any technology form created—eventually millions of dollars could be swindled from their gold creators, while the purple *business* people would gain from an obvious addition of product and *income*.

In the meantime, the strike caused the *productivity* of entertainment on network television to stop cold. The networks then
began to think about producing more reality shows, in which
many nonprofessionals create ideas for real people to "act out" in
gimmicky—and many times embarrassing—television programs
that have fewer creative rights or professional protections attached
to them. In other words, the *business* royalty of media moguls were
ready to produce product for which they had less expensive salaries
to pay and fewer royalties to shell out to competitive artists who
create it.

Sounds like another gainful *business* deal for purple people on
the short run; but in the long run, most reality shows don't tend
to have any shelf life. A television network would eventually dam-
age its long-term *productivity* if it found itself unable to repackage
syndication of a back list of old reality shows. In addition, certain
television actors are considered gold standard stars for a reason.
People like to see them perform. These supportive viewers attract
advertisers, and the advertisers tend to feel a lot more comfortable
about spending their money on proven stars and long-running
programs than with experimental reality shows.

Another aspect that added to the dilemma of television network *productivity* was the actors' support of the writers. As competitive artists and talented gold people themselves, the actors understood that without quality writing and production, they could
not have become stars. They agreed that the writers needed to
be paid fairly for their work. The actors also understood that
too many reality shows had the potential to put a strain on their
careers, and therefore, their ability to increase their own *income.*
Whereas the ordinary people who participate in reality shows are
happy just to be on TV, real actors still had to make a productive living. And as millions of television viewers and advertisers
became restless and disengaged with the loss of quality television programming, the purple people eventually chose to sign
off on a new agreement that would satisfy everyone, and get
them all back to creating marketable product that they all could
count on.

There is also such a thing as *overproduction*. What happens when a company or entrepreneur creates more product than a market supports? After a boom in American housing around the turn of the new millennium, a recent downturn in the economic marketplace has caused thousands of home foreclosures across the nation. As with all other industries, the investment in the product must still be accounted for. Just as retail and production companies are forced to offer massive discount sales to liquidate overstocks of slow-moving product, the banks and loans owners of home mortgages are forced to recoup their investments by reselling thousands of foreclosed homes to those who have the cash to buy them.

This market of foreclosures has now created a boom for those who invest in wholesale real estate, home repair, rental property management, foreclosure announcement lists, scouting, moving, truck rental, and various forms of real estate and foreclosure seminars. Many of the beneficiaries of these new *real estate* opportunities are green people: qualified salespeople, home and rental service providers, resell marketers, and organized middlemen who negotiate between the purple banks—who are looking to recoup their losses—and investors with cash and good credit who are looking to score deals on available homes.

In many cases of overproduction, an individual or company's miscalculation and loss can become a gain of *business* for someone else. The overabundance of goods is then recycled by those who are in position to take advantage of the downfall. Even an overproduction of automobiles can be sold by breaking down cars into their many parts: tires, engines, aluminum, brakes, car speakers, and so forth. Therefore, the overproduction of one company can create *productivity* for another. The product remains king, and without it there is no *business*.

So, how productive are you and your company? How many goods, products, services or viable ideas do you produce or still have that are idling on your to-do list? Either you create your own goods for *business*, or you negotiate to buy and resell or invest in someone else's goods, but *productivity* must be a part of your formula for continued success. There is no way around it.

Now, using the same *income* for each respective year of your Equation Chart, divide your personal *income* by the total amount that you or your company grossed from the sales of your personal or company services and/or products for the same respective year, and multiply it by 100 percent to find Your Value of Productivity.

PROGRESS

Webster's Third New International Dictionary provides the following meaning for the word *progress:* to make a journey, or to make a royal progress; to move forward, to proceed or advance from place to place, point to point, or step to step. *Progress* is also defined as development to a higher, better, or more advanced stage; to make continual improvements. And finally, it is simply to push forward.

One of the most striking examples of economic *progress* that comes to mind in the United States, the land of opportunity, is the business story of Madam C.J. Walker. *The Guinness Book of Records* cites her as the first female—black or white—to become a self-made millionaire. Born Sarah Breedlove in 1867, the daughter of former slaves in Louisiana, at the break of the twentieth century Walker turned her entrepreneurship in African-American hair care and preparation into an historic institution.

Married at age 14 to her first husband—Moses McWilliams, who was reportedly killed by a white lynch mob in Mississippi—Sarah took on the full name of her second husband, C.J. Walker, a newspaperman whose advertising and mail order knowledge contributed to the success of her hair-care *business.*

Uneducated in her youth, Walker learned to read and write as an adult and worked as a laundry woman to support her only daughter, A'Lelia, through college. Setting up *business* roots in St. Louis, Missouri—where her brothers worked as barbers—Madam Walker became afflicted with a scalp condition that caused her to lose some of her hair in her mid-thirties. She experimented with several home-based remedies, finally hitting on a scalp conditioning and healing formula. She called it "Madam Walker's Wonderful Hair Grower." To meet the needs of women who lacked running water, supplies, or equipment, Walker also created a hot comb with specially spaced teeth to soften and straighten black hair.

To market her groundbreaking products and hair-care methods, Walker targeted poor blacks in the rural south and southeast—who were often neglected by predominantly white hair-care and hair-product manufacturers. She soon became the first woman to sell products through mail order, and organized a nationwide membership of door-to-door agents, teaching her customers as well as her staff through personal demonstrations. Creating The Walker System, Madam C.J. established a hair culturist union, and—with the help of her daughter A'Lelia—went on to develop a chain of beauty parlors throughout the United States, the Caribbean, and South America that employed more than 3,000 people.

She later started the Lelia College of Beauty Culture in Pittsburgh, where she lived and worked with her daughter and staff from 1908 to 1910 to help other African-American women find gainful employment and personal pride in their accomplishments. Moving next to Indianapolis, Indiana, where she built the Madam C.J. Walker Manufacturing Company, Walker invested in African-American real estate, cultural theater, and night clubs, and provided financial backing for various community needs and programs. By 1914 her hair-care company had grossed more than a million dollars, and included perfumes, toothpaste, soap, powders, shampoo, and hair dressings and pomades.

Walker famously stated of her success, "I am a woman who came from the cotton fields of the South. From there I was promoted to the washtub. From there I was promoted to the cook kitchen. And from there I promoted myself into the business of manufacturing hair goods and preparations. I have built my own factory on my own ground" (*Africana Encyclopedia*, "Madam C.J. Walker/Hair and Beauty Culture").

Moving from her headquarters in Minneapolis and Indianapolis to Harlem, Walker's entrepreneurship and wealth would help fuel the Harlem Renaissance of African-American *business, art*, culture, education, and intellectual leadership of the 1920s. Building an immaculate house in Irvington, New York, known as "The Dark Tower" or Villa Lewaro—a 34-room mansion designed by Vetner Woodson Tandy, an African-American architect—Walker's homes and establishments were frequented by Harlem Renaissance notables until her death in 1919 when her daughter A'Lelia took over the helm of the *business*.

An energetic, hard-working, innovative, and fearless woman, Madam C.J. Walker left behind a legacy marked by *passion, commitment, dedication, loyalty, purpose, organization, productivity*, and above all, she established a strong example of *progress* for not only African-Americans, but for all who attempt to control their own economic destiny through entrepreneurship.

In more recent years, particularly in field of advanced technology, courageous entrepreneurs have pushed the world forward by leaps and bounds. Who could ever imagine what young engineers have been able to do with computer and Internet technology? From personal computers, to computer games, microchips, semiconductors, interactive software, computer graphics, advanced sound systems, to cell phones, and iPod download devices, the *progress* of advanced technology has been phenomenal. But we owe much of this *progress* in technology, not only to the young, gold engineers who continue to come up with creative ideas, but to the purple venture capitalists who back it.

New technology was not viewed as a *business* model on which traditional investors could place a straightforward price tag. Imagine telling a bank executive who makes his bread and butter investing in housing developments that you intend to create an Internet search engine to allow online customers faster access to all of the valuable information on the Web. Then imagine telling him that, although you have no prior *business* experience, you need $2 million for start-up. Good luck securing *that* deal! Many of the young computer wizards who offered such proposals were not even suit-and-tie guys who might convey a *business*-like appearance.

However, once Silicon Valley began to reward venture capitalists handsomely if they were game enough to invest, the young, college whiz types became new *attraction* magnets for high-percentage-gain investors. Whereas many of the young, computer engineers lacked traditional *business* management structure, a number of venture capitalists had enough experience in the worlds of finance and management to supply the necessary structure for the new technology startups. Hands-on management also allowed the investors opportunities to watch over the *progress* of the *business*, in order to safeguard their profits.

An explosion of technology billionaires ensued. The likes of Steve Jobs of Apple; Gordon E. Moore of Intel; William Hewlett and David Packard of Hewlett-Packard; Larry Ellison of Oracle; Thomas Siebel of Siebel Systems; David Duffield of PeopleSoft; James Clark of Netscape and Silicon Graphics; David Filo and Jerry Yang of Yahoo! Larry Page, Sergey Brin, and Eric Schmidt of Google; and of course, Bill Gates, Paul Allen, Steven Ballmer, and Charles Simonyi of Microsoft all found incredible success in these technological investments.

This list would be hundreds of names longer if I included those at the multimillionaire level. But it's not just about the *income* that these new-wave entrepreneurs have made; they have also created an amazing level of *progress* through the world's use of their new products. One has to understand that each and every one of these professionals had to *love* the *art* of computer engineering and innovation *first*, before he could ever attract the *support* of the financiers they needed to create a significant amount of *business*.

Although the purple venture capitalists who invested in these golden talents and others were definitely concerned with *income* and *productivity*—considering the many engineers who have joined the ranks of the venture capital game themselves—the *progress* and advancements of humanity in science have indeed advanced, especially in biotechnology. Venture capitalists have continued to put their funds on the lab tables for *progress* in human, plant, and animal organism research to help create the top biotechnology firms in the world. These new developments allow passionate scientists to continue their work to uncover ways for humans to live healthier and longer lives.

For those of you who are not scientifically astute, the question may be asked, "What exactly does biotechnology mean to the average human?" Well, cancer research, safer food processing, investigation of genetic diseases, DNA testing, genealogical study of family blood lines, metabolism studies for obesity, diabetes and stem cell research, improvement of farm crops and agriculture, energy enhancers, anti-aging products, improved vitamins, emotional disorder medicines, regeneration research for damaged animal and human organs, better protein research, continued HIV/AIDS treatments and study, and oncology products are all a part of the biotechnology world.

Although some of us may argue against too much human tampering with nature, the *business* of investing in scientific *progress* has allowed millions of us to live longer, safer, and much improved lives. And whether you agree with it or not, the *business* and *progress* of advance technology will indeed continue.

Now, if applicable, subtract both your Beginning Career Chart and your Decline Chart from your Career Prime to find your own

Value of Progress   and   Value of Decline

_____   _____

You may do the same to find the projected *progress* or Decline when moving from your Present Job to your Preferred Job and then on to your Dream Job.

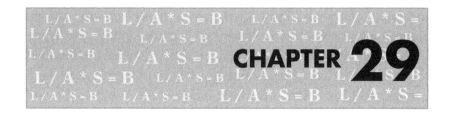

CHAPTER 29

POWER

Webster's Third New International Dictionary defines the word *power* as a position of ascendancy; ability to compel obedience; a large number or quantity; multitude; abundance; the capacity of acting or producing an effect; political sway; social sway; influence; prestige; a delegated right or privilege; prerogative; authority; ability to change legal relations; the ability to control; physical might or resources; strength; intensity; source or means of supplying energy; the time rate at which work is done or energy is emitted or transferred; and finally, magnification.

All the definitions of *power* have serious connotations. Where do we even begin with all of that? Well, for *business* purposes, I would begin with the *power* to do or the ability to make happen. In the case of this book, *power* denotes the ability to do *business*. One of the surest ways to create or acquire new *business* is to have the *power, income,* and *productivity* of a standing *business*. Powerful people tend to buy into, take over, and form new businesses regularly. This practice becomes a measure of increasing and maintaining *power*—as the definition states—in abundance or multitude.

Once *power* is attained, the popular saying "the sky is the limit" seems closer to reality. Someone who achieves great success begins to feel a lack of restrictions or limitations. Your wildest dreams become available, and your life opens up from its hard shell to reveal a pearl. This new *power* then serves to elevate the value of the individual, product, or company above the norm of a privately owned enterprise—where publicly invested funds are able to take the *business* to new heights. Such is the case on Wall Street—where company stock is traded to those with the *income power* to invest. Those who have the ability to invest—or to receive multiple investments—are indeed more powerful than those who cannot.

Barron's Dictionary of Business Terms defines this powerful investment tool, the Initial Public Offering (IPO), as a corporation's first offering of stock to the public. The investment in any enterprise that does well enough to become a corporation—eventually leading to a public stock offering—can make the initial owner extremely rich and the company as a whole, extremely profitable and influential. When the newly issued stock is in great public demand—with stock prices rocketing skyward, due to more demand than available shares—the *business* is then termed a *hot issue*. And the more shares you own, the more economic *power* you wield within the company.

At this level of entrepreneurship, the individual or company becomes recognized as an institution worthy of mass investment from the public—producing the strength and resources needed to effect a powerful *business movement*. The pooling of *income* and resources alone creates the necessary *power* to move.

In China, a nation of more than a billion citizens, an embrace of capitalism, driven by active stock exchanges in Hong Kong and Shanghai, has created the fastest and most intense twenty-first century *business* community in the world. Within the industries of intellectual technology (IT), manufacturing, and real estate, a number of Chinese businessmen and businesswomen have quickly made their marks, making China the second-largest nation of billionaires—behind the United States.

The publicly traded companies of Alibaba.com, PetroChina energy, the Industrial and Commercial Bank of China, Country Garden real estate, and many other enterprises have helped the

Shanghai Stock Exchange and the Hong Kong Stock Exchange to do tremendously well in building a powerful nation of new businesses, rivaling the American giants of Microsoft, Google, Exxon Mobil, and Citigroup. As a result of China's fluid investment activity, its various industries have sparked worldwide *business* interest as a nation to be reckoned with.

However, before we begin to consider the multi–billion-dollar empires of Chinese companies and others to be out of the reach of our personal and company goals, we must all understand that *power* is built and lost by individuals and companies who gain or lose the favor of massive groups of supporters. In China, as in any other nation, the key to becoming powerful is to build enterprises of sound value that are able to impact the largest group of followers.

The road toward legitimate *power* begins with the question, "How many people can I engage for business? How do I impact a thousand? How do I impact *ten* thousand? How do I impact *twenty* thousand?" You then continue to build a strategic network of staff, assistants, partners, customers, advisors, traders, and investors—with the ultimate goal of influencing the largest amount of people to back your expansion. Eventually—once your *business* system is firmly in place and projected to make profits—you evaluate your assets, create a viable price, and offer the public a piece of the pie.

This process rarely happens overnight. *Power* is usually attained by walking a steadily climbing road of strong *business* practices. Nevertheless, with new technology, such as the Internet, an audience of followers are able to move so swiftly in their support of a new enterprise that a rapid rise to *power* can seem almost instant, particularly within a nation as competitive, as driven, and as populated as China. Internet entrepreneurs are creating wealth and *power* in China by leaps and bounds.

Let's make no mistakes about it; real *power* is in the numbers—the amount of revenue created, the amount of revenue invested, and the amount of revenue distributed. This revenue creation, investment, and distribution manifest the ability of the upper *business* class to compel, to produce, to delegate, and to amass privilege and authority in every nation around the world. Once we are all able to calculate our own Business Energy—through *The Equation*—we will be able to assess exactly how close or how far away from *power* we really are. And if having the *power* to control your own destiny in *business* and in life is your goal, then the first step toward that change is knowing where you presently stand in the pecking order.

Although an Initial Public Offering or IPO, may be a more traditional route of producing massive *business power*—in the high-stakes competition to acquire wealth—is it not the only route.

Barron's Dictionary of Business Terms defines a *hedge fund* as a private investment partnership in which the general partner has made a substantial, personal investment, and whose offering memorandum allows for the fund to take both long and short positions, use leverage and derivatives, and invest in many markets, often taking large risks on speculative strategies.

With some hedge fund accounts, investors allow the account brokers to use the funds in whatever methods possible to make gains. Only those with the economic *power* to invest millions of dollars or more are even invited to the table, producing funds that added—and multiplied—up to $1 trillion in managed capital. That's *$1 trillion* invested—a phenomenal pool of *income power*.

Despite the original concept—which was to conservatively protect investors from the ups and downs of the stock market—hedge funds became the most powerful and intense forms of investment packages ever created. The funds have also proven to be the most profitable, landing countless new members on the Forbes 400 list faster than ever.

The idea of the hedge fund was first conceived by *Fortune* magazine editor and sociologist Alfred Winslow Jones as early as 1949. It allowed Jones to outperform top mutual funds in the mid 1960s by more than 85 percent. He simultaneously took 1 percent of the funds assets for a management fee, and a hefty 20 percent of its profits each year. With his frequent success, the rush of the rich to become richer through use of hedge funds was on.

However, with their particular selections of investments or strategies, not many hedge fund managers enjoyed the same success that Jones did, and multiple funds collapsed in the late 1960s. The idea lost its luster with investors—luster that was later resurrected by the Hungarian-born billionaire George Soros and his Quantum Fund.

Soros, a nomadic opportunist in banking and finance, read relentlessly about the global marketplace. He utilized an army of paid informants who worked in central banks and on trading desks around the world. His widespread, covert style of gathering information led to accusations of insider trading on multiple occasions. Nevertheless, Soros and his Quantum Fund went on to earn shareholders returns in excess of 30 percent for more than three decades. Soros has managed to collect billions for himself in the process, and has suffered only two major losses—in Britain and Russia—before retiring recently to concentrate his influence on international politics and environmental issues.

Soros still stands as the wealthiest hedge fund manager on the *Forbes* list, at more than $8 billion, and he has reopened the gates for hundreds of new hedge fund managers to follow. Since his retirement, his two sons continue to run the family *business* of flipping investment capital. If you can afford the long-money ride and the uncertainty, hedge funds can supply another healthy infusion of capital and *power*.

In fact, the *power* of investment and finance has now replaced various other methods of acquiring fast and influential wealth. Through the stock markets—not only in China, but around the world—individuals and companies like George Soros and his Quantum Fund are creating *power* for themselves by investing in the lucrative stock of other successful businesses and projects. These purple investors are then able to live the lifestyles of privilege, luxury, and security that we *all* desire. So my advice to us all—in order to increase our own economic *power* in the years to come—is to learn the game of investments, while building the strength, *consistency*, and profitability of our new or existing companies to make them worth investing in.

In final section, "The Equation in Use," you may now compare your Value of Income to your Value of Productivity. Where do you lose or gain your percentage points of *power?*

Value of Income　　　　and　　　　Value of Productivity

_____　　　　　_____

What does the difference in these two numbers mean to the value of your overall *business?* Sometimes we are better off working under the framework of the company . . . and sometimes not. The key is to figure out how to make them both work for us—*or* how to utilize the best economic options of *power* that fit our *income* and character. And by all means—if you can manage to save enough to afford it—learn to partner with and invest in the people and companies that have larger *productivity* and profit than your own.

RESPONSIBILITY

We have now reached the twentieth and final element of *The Equation* in *business*. If you are fortunate enough to become wealthy—at any level—in your own *business* life, how responsible will you be with your own *income, productivity, progress,* and *power?* What would then become your new mission and goals in life?

Webster's Third New International Dictionary defines the word *responsibility* as the quality or state of being responsible with moral, legal or mental accountability. *Responsibility* is also characterized as reliability, trustworthiness and the ability to pay; something for which anyone is accountable. Its root word, *responsible,* is simply defined as likely to be called upon to answer.

I once read an anthropology book on a Native American culture in which—within certain tribes—the wealthiest chiefs of each new crop year would throw elaborate and festive parties for the rest of their tribesmen. They would then be honored by the opportunity to give away all of their wealth to begin a new crop year. Reared in a capitalistic system— where I had learned early on to save and keep money—I first viewed this elaborate, tribal party idea as crazy! *You work that hard just give your wealth all away?*

But as I continued to read, I found that the same group of hard-working chiefs would usually become the wealthiest tribesmen each year, until they became too old to compete with the younger chiefs. So it was pretty much expected within the tribe that—even though the wealthiest chiefs would give away their assets at the end of each crop year—these celebrated chiefs would likely collect it all back. They were essentially celebrating their individual *power* to build and then give, and their community would love them all the more for it. However, you could only acquire that *power* of *responsibility* through working hard to attain excess wealth in the first place. And any chief who was able to throw the most end-of-crop-year celebrations would become a legend.

In many present-day societies, it has become a normal practice for the concerned rich to give back to the community through their charitable foundations. Oprah Winfrey, in her purple status, is hardly the first or the last to give. John D. Rockefeller gave millions of his wealth to benefit the arts, education, architecture, scientific research, and more.

Instead of passing down all of his wealth to his children, Conrad Hilton—the founder of the Hilton Hotel empire—committed the bulk of his wealth to creating the Conrad N. Hilton Foundation, with the goal of alleviating worldwide suffering. The foundation—established in 1944—began a Humanitarian Prize in 1996.

Andrew Carnegie—the longtime business rival of John D. Rockefeller—established his chain of national libraries and gave away millions of his fortune to support education.

Noted comedian, entertainer, and educator Bill Cosby has given millions of his wealth to charity for educational purposes. Boxing promoter Don King has made a practice of giving millions to the United Negro College Fund through donations from championship boxing matches. Walter Annenberg of the *Philadelphia Inquirer* newspaper empire gave more than $1 billion to the public school system and educational programming for television. Media mogul Ted Turner pledged a billion dollars to the efforts of the United Nations. Donald Trump regularly donates his public speaking fees, which are often valued at more than three hundred thousand dollars per event, to charitable causes. The Walton family of the Wal-Mart empire have all pledged hundreds of millions of dollars of their wealth to educational programs and have established the Children's Scholarship Fund. George Soros—the Hedge Fund mogul discussed in Chapter 29—has, by himself, given away billions of dollars globally to affect international politics, including funds towards reconstructing education in South Africa and rebuilding the Soviet Union.

To top them all, Berkshire Hathaway's multibillionaire investor Warren Buffett—who had not been known as a philanthropist—decided to pledge more than $60 billion of his personal fortune to the Bill and Melinda Gates Foundation at a rate of $1.5 billion a year, on top of the estimated $30 billion in assets that Gates and his wife had already pledged. That's nearly a $100 billion in charity from just two men—before more donations were added to their pot. Microsoft co-founder Bill Gates has since retired from his leadership position within the company—allowing his friend and long-time business partner Steven Ballmer to take over—so that he can focus all of his time and efforts on charitable causes.

Like the example of the Native American chiefs of centuries ago, the desire of the super-rich to step away from the steady grind of *business* and become career philanthropists is a socially redeeming and satisfying practice. When people have amassed more wealth than they could ever spend in one lifetime, the continued accumulation of that wealth can indeed become meaningless. However, the dissemination of that wealth creates a new *purpose*, esteem, a worthwhile goal, and a larger legacy. Philanthropy expands the wealth further, thereby increasing its significance within a local, national or worldwide community.

An individual or company can never expect to amass an excess of *income* and *power* in any field without first inspiring millions of supporters—all whom may eventually ask for advice, a helping hand, or an investment into their own ideas. And if any of the super-rich were to honestly claim that no one has invested time, effort, advise and hard work into them, their company, and their ideas—then I would forever excuse them of their *responsibility* to the supportive public. But realistically, since no millionaire or billionaire alive or dead could ever claim to have earned their wealth entirely by their own efforts, it is very obvious that they owe plenty of gratitude to the millions who have supported their efforts, products, and services. In fact, the richer you are, the more people you owe, and therefore, the more *responsibility* you will have to others.

It is the same *responsibility* that those in positions of royalty have owed to their subjects since the beginning of time, from pharaohs, emperors, kings, queens, chiefs, lords, parliament, and clergy; and the same *responsibility* that all government officials—president, vice president, chancellor, governor, senator, legislator, mayor, council member—owe to their constituents. Even tyrants must be responsible to the degree that they must maintain the population over which they have dominion. And if a tyrant has no *responsibility* to a people, then he is a ruler of no one.

In fact, no one individual governs any large number of people. Instead, they employ officials who carry out the duties and enforcement of their reign. Each one of these officials has a *responsibility* to a certain group, area, or number of citizens, like *responsibility* the various managers within a company have to its staff of employees. If those officials, guards, and managers have the *responsibility* of overseeing a body of people, that leads to the next question: Who has the *responsibility* of overseeing *them?*

No matter what economic or political philosophy each nation may follow, humanity and civilization—like a stand of DNA—remain as links of an interlocking chain. And no matter how important a link we think we are in that chain, we are all still connected to it. So it becomes paramount for each individual to use every facility available to him or her in order to strengthen the links of that chain for the betterment of us all. However, this is not a forced choice, but a personal one. No one can make a rich man or woman want to give to the common cause of humanity; they must *want* to. But we must *all* understand—as individual entrepreneurs, corporate executives, or rank and file of a company—that a healthy economic community creates more opportunities of *support* for everyone, whereas a weakened community creates hesitancy, ineffectiveness, and panic.

Ultimately, the *responsibility* to maintain a healthy and progressive community makes sense for *business*. This is why I have chosen to write and publish this book: to strengthen the universal understanding of how *love, art, support,* and *business* all connect to create an ongoing and worldwide industry of human *progress*. As a creative thinker, writer, and entrepreneur—who is most concerned about the literate and economic well-being of our international community—I accept my role of *responsibility* to inform you, my family, my associates, and my partners and friends about this universal formula of *The Equation* and how it can be utilized to create personal and company success for everyone. Now what do *you* accept as *your responsibility?*

THE EQUATION IN USE

$L/A*S=B$

Summing up the details of academic education, evaluations of various enterprises, successful case studies, and a multitude of personal business decisions and activity, the complete formula of *The Equation* became this: *Love / Art * Support = Business* or $L / A * S = B$, as well as *Red / Gold * Green = Purple*. I then began to test the idea in lectures as early as 1997 for those who *love* (or hate) their occupations, who increased their skills of *art* within their respective fields (or did not), who created a momentum of *support* for their goods and services (or failed to), and therefore was able to produce successful *business* (or was unable to).

In this chapter, I present two options for an individual or company's application of *The Equation*. Option #1 is a personal estimate that can be used to make a quick and easy assessment of your individual or company Equation Chart. The goal of Option #1 is to determine a basic idea of where you stand in your career, or where your company stands within its industry. If you or your company possess (or lack) strengths in the basic elements of personal or company *love, passion, commitment, dedication, loyalty,* and *consistency* in your present work space, or within your present industry, Option #1 will reveal it within The Passion Chart, and your assessment can be symbolized as having strong or weak "Red."

If you or your company is proficient in, or lack, certain practical skills, advancements in technology, inspired creativity, or specific goals that influence your proficiency in *art, adoration, presentation, purpose, execution,* or *excellence,* your honest chart numbers will reveal as much in the Competitive Rank Chart, and can be symbolized as having strong or weak "Gold." An added note on rankings is that those who work for themselves or at smaller companies have an obvious rank advantage, as will be explained in detail below within *adoration.*

If you or your company has, or has not, amassed the necessary amount of *support,* through *attraction, packaging, organization, imagery,* and *movement* to increase your market audience, your honest market share will be revealed within your Supportive Range Chart, and can be symbolized by strong or weak "Green."

And if you or your company has been able, or not able, to make successful *business* transactions which lead to *income, productivity, progress, power,* and a greater *responsibility* to the surrounding community that supports you, such will be reflecting in your final calculations of Business Energy, and can symbolized by strong or weak "Purple."

Option #1 provides the bare and personal estimates. However, for individuals and or companies who may desire a more in-depth analysis of their Equation Chart, Option #2 may be more suitable. Option #2 asks that you utilize real data and provide more objective surveys from individuals outside of yourself or your company. With Option #2, more accurate and researched numbers are used instead of the personal estimates that were utilized in Option #1. In other words, for Option #2, what is the objective view of your career success outside of your personal assessment, or the objective view of your company's success outside of its internal assessment?

You could also utilize *both* options, depending on how serious and intent you are on improving your personal career or company performance.

So let us now begin. Print out *The Equation* Chart from *www.TheEquationBook.com* or create your own using the sample provided in Figure 31.1.

The Equation Chart	L (Love)	/	A (Art)	= QN	*	S (Support)	=	B (Business)	Income Value	Productivity Value
Option #1 Option #2	Red (N)		Gold (D)	Quotient Number		Green (RSN)		Purple (BEN)	$\frac{\text{Income}}{(\text{BEN})} * 100\%$	$\frac{\text{Income}}{\text{Company}} * 100\%$
Present Job, Career, Goal										
Preferred Job, Career, Goal										
Dream Job, Career, Goal										
Career Beginning										
Career Peak										
Career Decline										

Figure 31.1   The Equation Chart (blank)

THE PASSION CHART

For the Red Section of *The Equation*, use The Passion Chart supplied (*www.TheEquationBook.com*), or create a chart of six columns of your own to represent your Present Job, Career, or Company Goals; your Preferred Job, Career or Company Goals; and your Dream Job, Career, or Company Goals (where applicable); as well as the Beginning, Peak, and Decline of your personal career or company history (where applicable). You may also create your own charts to apply to any business year, any career goal, or any specific time period. This is now your chance to be creative and apply *The Equation* to your own business needs and assessments. (See Figures 31.2 and 31.3.)

PASSION

On a scale of 1 to 20, with 1 being the least passionate and 20 being the most passionate, how would you honestly rate your

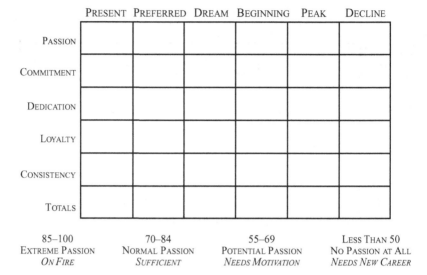

	PRESENT	PREFERRED	DREAM	BEGINNING	PEAK	DECLINE
PASSION						
COMMITMENT						
DEDICATION						
LOYALTY						
CONSISTENCY						
TOTALS						

85–100	70–84	55–69	LESS THAN 50
EXTREME PASSION	NORMAL PASSION	POTENTIAL PASSION	NO PASSION AT ALL
ON FIRE	*SUFFICIENT*	*NEEDS MOTIVATION*	*NEEDS NEW CAREER*

Figure 31.2   The Passion Chart (blank)

	PRESENT	PREFERRED	DREAM	BEGINNING	PEAK	DECLINE
PASSION	15	18	12	19	19	13
COMMITMENT	8	19	8	19	19	8
DEDICATION	15	18	12	19	19	13
LOYALTY	8	19	8	19	19	8
CONSISTENCY	15	19	10	19	19	13
TOTALS	61	93	50	95	95	55

85–100	70–84	55–69	LESS THAN 50
EXTREME PASSION	NORMAL PASSION	POTENTIAL PASSION	NO PASSION AT ALL
ON FIRE	*SUFFICIENT*	*NEEDS MOTIVATION*	*NEEDS NEW CAREER*

Figure 31.3   The Passion Chart (filled in)

personal ability, or your company's ability, to sacrifice and suffer, surrender to displays of excitement, have enthusiasm and devotion to your personal career or the company goals that you believe in?

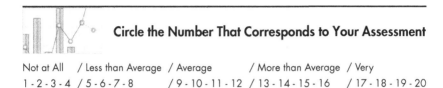

Circle the Number That Corresponds to Your Assessment

Not at All / Less than Average / Average   / More than Average / Very
1 - 2 - 3 - 4 / 5 - 6 - 7 - 8   / 9 - 10 - 11 - 12 / 13 - 14 - 15 - 16   / 17 - 18 - 19 - 20

You may fill in your *passion* rating in the respective columns (where applicable). Review the sample (Figure 31.3).

COMMITMENT

On a scale of 1 to 20, with 1 being the least committed and 20 being the most committed, rate your pledge to follow through on your personal or company goals, with or without pay, while obligated to a moral choice and a definite course of action.

How committed are you to believe in your personal or company goals?

You may fill in your *commitment* rating in the respective columns below your *passion* numbers (where applicable).

DEDICATION

On a scale of 1 to 20, with 1 being the least dedicated and 20 being the most dedicated, rate your personal ability, or the ability of your company, to sacrifice time, effort, creativity, land, and or capital for the attainment of your personal or company goals.

In other words, now that you've assessed your *passion* and *commitment*, how much are you willing to sacrifice from your personal life or your company's normal operations to prioritize toward a single goal?

You may fill in your *dedication* rating in the respective columns below your *commitment* numbers (where applicable).

LOYALTY

On a scale of 1 to 20, with 1 being the least loyal and 20 being the most loyal, how would you honestly rate your ability to remain faithful and unswerving in allegiance? How would you rate your fidelity or tenacious adherence to the principles and practices of your goal? How much are you willing to agree with a company platform or program in regard to your career? And how would you rate your ability to maintain that *loyalty* through good times and bad?

You may fill in your *loyalty* rating in the respective columns below your *dedication* numbers (where applicable).

CONSISTENCY

On a scale of 1 to 20, with 1 being the least consistent and 20 being the most consistent, how would you honestly rate your personal ability, or the ability of your company to maintain a high level of performance, while adhering to a singleness of purpose that is in harmony with all your goals?

Can you or your company be counted on to perform consistently at a high level that settles the anxieties of others? This is what is meant to have *consistency*.

You or your company can always be counted on to get the job done. You may fill in your *consistency* rating in the respective columns below your *loyalty* numbers (where applicable).

Now add up the numbers in each column and place the totals in their proper places within *The Equation* Chart from (*www.TheEquation Book.com*) in the first Love (L), Red, or Numerator (N) column.

Review the sample (Figure 31.1).

You have now completed the first section of *The Equation* Chart. Option #1 is your personal and honest assessment based on gross estimates. Either you or your company has *passion, commitment, dedication, loyalty,* and *consistency* to produce the necessary amount of *love* to succeed in your personal career or company goals—or you don't. Assess your strength of "Red" accordingly.

However, for Option #2, you or your company need to survey others—both inside the company and outside the company (whoever is relevant)—about your personal or company performance in these same areas of *passion, commitment, dedication, loyalty,* and *consistency* to create a more objective average. For Option #2, you may print out as many Passion Charts as needed and share the definitions, questions, and ratings with those you intend to survey.

Also, to gather viable data for Option #2, the people you ask to assess your career or company in this survey need to be aware of your personal Career, your company Goals, and your business History (where applicable).

To ask individuals who have no real knowledge of your Career, Goals or History would be fruitless. And to ask individuals with only optimistic or glowing reviews of your personal career or company performance would be just as ineffective. So the goal for Option #2 clearly becomes a search for informed objectivity from your business or industry peers.

COMPETITIVE RANK CHART

For the Gold Section of *The Equation,* use the Competitive Rank Chart (*www.TheEquationBook.com*), or create your own. For your Competitive Rank Chart, you will rank your personal or company skill or *art* within your given field. Option #1 will again be based on personal estimates, whereas the information provided for Option #2 will be measured by actual data. (See Figures 31.4 and 31.5.)

ADORATION

Within 5 general ranking groups, on a scale from 1 to 50, rank the recognition, worship, reverence or honor that you or your company receives within your respective industry for your skills, services, or products.

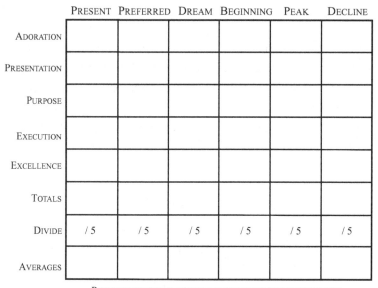

	PRESENT	PREFERRED	DREAM	BEGINNING	PEAK	DECLINE
ADORATION						
PRESENTATION						
PURPOSE						
EXECUTION						
EXCELLENCE						
TOTALS						
DIVIDE	/ 5	/ 5	/ 5	/ 5	/ 5	/ 5
AVERAGES						

ROUND AVERAGES UP OR DOWN TO THE NEAREST WHOLE NUMBER.

1–3	4–7	8–12	LESS THAN 13
GOLD STANDARD	SILVER	BRONZE	SHOWING UP
THE BEAST	*ABOVE AVERAGE*	*ON THE RADAR*	*OFF THE RADAR*

Figure 31.4   Competitive Rank Chart (blank)

	PRESENT	PREFERRED	DREAM	BEGINNING	PEAK	DECLINE
ADORATION	1-5	1-15	1-25	1-30	1-3	1-7
PRESENTATION	1-4	1-15	1-50	1-30	#1	1-4
PURPOSE	1-3	1-15	1-25	1-5	#1	1-5
EXECUTION	1-2	1-5	1-50	1-30	#1	1-7
EXCELLENCE	1-5	1-5	1-50	1-30	1-3	1-5
TOTALS	19	55	200	125	9	28
DIVIDE	/ 5	/ 5	/ 5	/ 5	/ 5	/ 5
AVERAGES	4	11	40	25	2	6

ROUND AVERAGES UP OR DOWN TO THE NEAREST WHOLE NUMBER.

1–3	4–7	8–12	LESS THAN 13
GOLD STANDARD	SILVER	BRONZE	SHOWING UP
THE BEAST	*ABOVE AVERAGE*	*ON THE RADAR*	*OFF THE RADAR*

Figure 31.5   Competitive Rank Chart (filled in)

This is where your personal or company's reputation is measured. Where do you rank among the staff, individuals or companies within your field?

	Circle the Number That Corresponds to Your Assessment			
Gold	/ Top 5	/ Top 10	/ Top 20	/ Top 50
# 1	/ 1 out of 5	/ 1 out of 10	/ 1 out of 20	/ 1 out of 50

You may fill in your *adoration* rating in the respective columns (where applicable). Review the sample (Figure 31.5).

As noted earlier, those who work for themselves or at smaller companies have an obvious rank advantage. But if you work at a larger company, rank yourself within your specific department. Your rank would then be 1 out of as many employees who work in the same field. And unless you know for a fact that you are indeed #1 in your department, rank yourself according to the number of staff members you are in direct competition with, for instance, 1 out of 8, which would place you within the Top 10.

If you are a manager or a supervisor, rank yourself among the others who hold a similar position. Within larger companies, franchises, and chain store industries, there may be a number of local, regional, and national managers and supervisors. In Option #1 of *The Equation* Chart, you may rank yourself based on the numbers you are aware of. But for the more detailed and accurate Option #2, find the data of the real number of managers and supervisors within your industry, and rank your level of *adoration* accordingly.

For all companies, partners, owners, producers directors, professional athletes, entertainers, and independent specialists, rank yourself among those you are in immediate competition with for *adoration* in your particular position. For Option #1, rank yourself within a general idea of where you stand. But for Option #2, use the real data that establishes the pecking order of your field, including recent surveys of Top 10 and Top 100 lists, or other common indexes of rank. And again, unless you know for a fact that you are #1, rank yourself based on the number of others you are in direct competition with.

In fields where competitive ranks of *art* can be broken down into *communal, local, regional, national,* or *world* population bases, rank yourself where you place. If you are unable to gauge your rank of competition on a *regional* or *national* level, then rank yourself within your smaller *communal* or *local* area, according to its respective population size.

For example; unless a barber or a hairdresser has *national* clients or a nationally known franchise, it makes no sense to try and determine ranking within the context of the thousands of barbers or hairdressers around the nation. However, if it is your goal to attract *national* clients and to form a *national* franchise, then for Option #2, find data to document the ranks among those in the *national* position that you or your company desires. The same goes for any other profession that can be broken down into geographical populations.

PRESENTATION

Are you one of the competitive leaders who present new products, goals, or services to your company, to the business community, or to the general public? Have you or your company received contracts, awards, advances, grants, or any form of recognized *presentation* to celebrate your personal, company, or team achievements? How would you rank your *presentation* value in your particular field among your competitors?

In other words, how would you rank your preparation and worthiness to pitch new ideas, products, services, performances, or your worthiness to receive awards for ideas, products, or performances that you or your company has introduced?

You may fill in your *presentation* rating in the respective columns below your *adoration* rank (where applicable).

Option #1 is based on what you immediately know. Option #2 is based on the real industry data that you research on the various *presentations* within your field.

PURPOSE

What is the *purpose* you have set for yourself or in your career or company? How would you rank your personal or company aim to keep that *purpose* in view with any plan, measure, exertion, or operation as compared to those in competition around you?

How do you or your team, company, or community benefit from your goals? How would you rank your specific *purpose*, or the *purpose* of your company, against those of your competitors?

You may fill in your rank of *purpose* in the respective columns below your rank of *presentation* (where applicable).

Option #1 is based on what you immediately know. Option #2 is based on industry research of the various ideas of *purpose* within your field. Do you know the *purpose* of your competitors? In Option #2, you would find out and create objective surveys to rank yourself in relation to them.

EXECUTION

Do you or your company exhibit effective *execution*? Rank your personal or company *execution* in your particular field as compared to those around you.

You may fill in your *execution* rating in the respective columns below your rank of *purpose* (where applicable).

Option #1 is based on what you immediately know. Option #2 is based on real industry data and surveys of individual and company *execution* within your field.

EXCELLENCE

Do you think you or your company has reached the point of *excellence* in achieving your goals? Rank your standings as compared to the *excellence* of the individual competitors or companies in your respective field? You may fill in your *excellence* rating in the respective columns below your rating for *execution* (where applicable).

Option #1 is based on what you immediately know. Option #2 is based on real industry data and surveys of individual and company *excellence* within your field.

You may now calculate your rank average for each respective column by adding up each competition number. For examples, 1 out of 8 would add the 8, and 1 out of 42 would add the 42. Divide the totals of each column by five. Then place the averages in their proper places within *The Equation* Chart in the second column of Art (A), Gold, or Denominator (D). Assess your strength of "Gold" accordingly.

Review the sample (Figure 31.1).

QUOTIENT NUMBER

Now that you have found you respective numbers of Red Love (L) and Gold Art (A), or your Numerator and Denominator of *The Equation* Chart, you may now find your Quotient Number (QN) by dividing your Numerator by your Denominator and place them within their respective third column under Quotient Number.

A Note on QN Readings: The higher your Quotient Number, the higher your position within your respective field. As your QN changes from each Job, Career, or Company Goal from Beginnings, Peaks, and Declines (where applicable), you are now able to gauge your strengths and weaknesses to design effective goals of improvement or to plan a full change of direction.

Supportive Range Chart

For the Green Section of *The Equation*, use the Supportive Range Chart (*www.TheEquationBook.com*) or create your own.

Although many us may be overzealous in our assessments of *passion* or Red Love and our ratings of competition or Gold Art within our respective Jobs, Careers, or Company Goals, as well as *business* histories, it is much more difficult to fabricate numbers for the assessment of Green Support. The true measure of impact

	PRESENT	PREFERRED	DREAM	BEGINNING	PEAK	DECLINE
ATTRACTION						
PACKAGING						
ORGANIZATION						
IMAGERY						
MOVEMENT						
TOTALS						
DIVIDE	/ 5	/ 5	/ 5	/ 5	/ 5	/ 5
AVERAGES						
MULTIPLY	10%	10%	10%	10%	10%	10%
TOTALS						

ROUND THE FINAL TOTALS UP OR DOWN TO THE NEAREST THOUSAND.

COMMUNAL	LOCAL	REGIONAL	NATIONAL	WORLD
10,000S OR LESS	100S OF THOUSANDS	MILLIONS	10S OF MILLIONS	100S OF MILLIONS

Figure 31.6   Supportive Range Chart (blank)

your *business* has on those it services cannot be judged by your individual or internal company opinions, but by gathering the *support* of teammates and customers through *attraction, packaging, organization, imagery,* and *movement.* (See Figures 31.6 and 31.7.)

ATTRACTION

For readers to complete *The Equation* Chart in Option #1, you are allowed to estimate, within reason, what range of people you are able to reach and attract in *support* of your career, products, services, or those of your company. But for Option #2, please record the real marketing data. That data would include radio advertisement numbers, print ad numbers, television appearances, published interviews, sponsorships, Internet marketing, making

	PRESENT	PREFERRED	DREAM	BEGINNING	PEAK	DECLINE
ATTRACTION	6,000,000	10,000,000	39,000,000	500,000	15,000,000	8,000,000
PACKAGING	1,000,000	5,000,000	7,500,000	200,000	10,000,000	2,000,000
ORGANIZATION	12,000,000	15,000,000	30,000,000	2,000,000	8,000,000	12,000,000
IMAGERY	500,000	50,000,000	15,000,000	200,000	5,000,000	2,000,000
MOVEMENT	80,000	400,000	5,000,000	15,000	180,000	100,000
TOTALS	19,580,000	80,400,000	87,500,000	2,915,000	38,180,000	30,100,000
DIVIDE	/ 5	/ 5	/ 5	/ 5	/ 5	/ 5
AVERAGES	3,916,000	16,080,000	17,500,000	583,000	7,636,000	6,020,000
MULTIPLY	10%	10%	10%	10%	10%	10%
TOTALS	392,000	1,608,000	1,750,000	58,000	764,000	602,000

ROUND THE FINAL TOTALS UP OR DOWN TO THE NEAREST THOUSAND.

COMMUNAL	LOCAL	REGIONAL	NATIONAL	WORLD
10,000s OR LESS	100s OF THOUSANDS	MILLIONS	10s OF MILLIONS	100s OF MILLIONS

Figure 31.7   Supportive Range Chart (filled in)

the popular scene, or any other for where you are able to provide definite numbers. If you or your company utilizes no forms of *attraction*, which means you go home and go to bed after work, with no reason for anyone to know you, your company, or your products and or services, then please mark your *attraction* numbers accordingly.

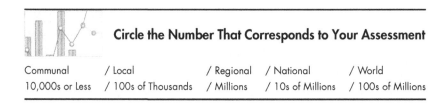

Circle the Number That Corresponds to Your Assessment

Communal	/ Local	/ Regional	/ National	/ World
10,000s or Less	/ 100s of Thousands	/ Millions	/ 10s of Millions	/ 100s of Millions

Fill in your range of *attraction* in the respective columns (where applicable). Review the sample (Figure 31.7).

PACKAGING

Thinking of all the combined values of your personal and or company skills, goals, products, and services, what range of people have you earnestly offered a packaged deal to?

If you or your company does not offer deals of your skills, services, or products, then answer accordingly. Fill in your range of *packaging* in the respective columns under your *attraction* rating (where applicable).

Whether you have chosen to use Option #1 or Option #2, the numbers you insert for *packaging* will be basically the same. It is much easier to determine how many people you have pitched a packaged deal to. *Packaging* is more than just placing your brand, products, goals, and/or services in front of people. *Packaging* is pitching them to move on a great deal or at least to get involved. So either you have pitched to a range of people in your marketing plans or you haven't. There are no made-up estimates to report here. If you or your company has not pitched a package, then select *communal* and record the proper number.

ORGANIZATION

There are plenty of *teams* involved in major *business* moves, whether or not we see those teams or give them much credit. So with the *organization* teamwork of personal friends, family, *business* associates, professional networks, or those of your company in mind, determine what range of people your team is able attract and garner *support* from.

Fill in your *organization* ratings in the respective columns under your *packaging* numbers (where applicable).

In Option #1, you are again allowed to estimate. But in Option #2, attempt to record the actual data regarding the number of people your *organization* is able to reach to elicit *support* of your *business*. However, since you may add the estimates of *support* from your team of business associates, it will be difficult to ensure accuracy for an *organization*. However, clearly, the *support* of a group will usually outnumber the *support* of an individual.

IMAGERY

As explained within the text, the *imagery* of brands, logos, people, places, products, memorable slogans, stylish fashion, showcases of wealth, and so on, are all parts of attracting *support* for *business*. *Imagery* numbers would include your personal or company sponsorships, as well as celebrity endorsement deals that help promote your personal or company brand and products. So what range of individuals have you actively influenced with your *imagery*?

If you or your company has no effective brand, logo, slogan, or *imagery* to connect a large range of people to *support* you, or you have not *used* your *imagery* to drive that *support*, then answer accordingly.

Fill in your *imagery* rating in the respective columns under your *organization* rating (where applicable).

In Option #1, even though *imagery* is a conscious effort, similar to *packaging*, the rating you will assign is still more of an estimate than an exact number. In certain cases, a popular person can affect an audience with a simple dress code, a certain car, or even by wearing certain colors. Therefore, we must take all of the various iterations into consideration. However, in Option #2, attempt to calculate the actual data of marketing or promotional activities that you or your company employ that may help promote the recognition and *imagery* of your brand, logo, services, products, or public appeal.

MOVEMENT

Now record the number of people who have actually been *moved* to *support* your personal or company goals, products, or services. As I explained with the rank of *art*, if you do not have a *regional* or *national* rank, then do not claim a *regional* or *national movement*. Record the most accurate number of people who have bought your products, used your services, or gotten involved to organize for your *support*, or for the *support* of your company.

Fill in the range of *movement* in the respective columns under your *imagery* rating (where applicable).

As with *packaging*, Option #1 and Option #2 for *movement* will be basically the same number of individuals who have actively supported you or your company. The only difference here is a quick estimate range of Option #1, as opposed to the real numbers of Option #2. And hopefully, your Option #1 estimates will not land miles away from the truth.

You may now calculate your Representative of Support Number(s) by adding up each column and dividing the totals by five to compute your Average of Support. However, since the range of *attraction, packaging, organization,* and *imagery* will hardly represent the number of people who are actually moved to *support* you or your company, we apply the 10 Percent Rule, which dictates that *any person or company that is able to move at least 10 percent of the people who are familiar with their goals, products, services or brand, is doing well.* If you or your company is able to move *more* than 10 percent, then consider it gravy.

Using the 10 Percent Rule, multiply your averages in the Supportive Range Chart by 10 percent, or 0.1, to compute your RSN Totals, then place the Totals in their proper places within *The Equation* Chart in the fourth column of Support (S), Green, or (RSN). Assess your strength of "Green" accordingly.

Now you may calculate your Business Equivalent Number (BEN) by multiplying your Quotient Number by your RSN Totals as documented below:

$$QN * RSN = BEN$$

Once you have calculated your Business Equivalent Number(s), place them in their respective places within *The Equation* Chart the fifth column of Business (B), Purple, or (BEN). Assess your strength of "Purple" accordingly.

Review the sample (Figure 31.1).

Your Business Equivalent Number (BEN) is based on how much *business* you or your company could possibly generate based on the documented *love*, your competitive rank of *art*, and the number of people who may *support* you in your specific Job, Career, or Goal at the Beginning, Peak, and or Peak of your career (where applicable). That Business Equivalent Number (BEN) is the force or amount of simple Business Energy (BE) that you or your company has created.

Simply speaking, you cannot expect much progressive response to your *business* if you have not put forth the relevant Business Energy that you or your company needs to succeed in your goals. No matter what you may hear or believe to the contrary, the consistency of successful business does not create itself. The production of Business Energy through *love*, *art*, and *support* is what creates that consistent success. Generally speaking, the more Business Energy (BE) you produce, the more valuable you become to yourself, your partners, your teammates, and your company. And those individuals and companies who produce *income* from a maximum of *business energy* will become the most successful in *purple business*.

With use of the calculated BEN(s) or Business Energy for your Present, Preferred, or Dream Job, Career, or Company Goals(where applicable), as well as the Beginning, Peak, and Peak of your *business* history, we are now able to compute your percentages of Income Value, Productivity Value, direction of *progress*, as well as discuss ideas to increase your personal and or company *power* and overall *responsibility* to the surrounding communities that *support* you.

INCOME VALUE

To find your Income Value for each respective Job, Career, Goal, or History, divide your actual Income or company Revenue by the respective Business Energy (BEN) in column five, then multiply by 100 percent as documented below.

Income or Revenue / (BEN) * 100% = Income Value

For Preferred and Dream Careers and Goals, estimate how much Business Energy (BEN) you believe you or your company could produce as well as how much Income or Revenue you believe you or your company could amass in that particular change of Career or Goal.

Your Income Value for each respective year in each Career or Goal will tell you precisely how much of your Business Energy you were able to take advantage of. Again, the 10 Percent Rule applies as good business. So anything above 10 percent is gravy.

With Income Value, we will find that some of us can be grossly underpaid or grossly overpaid from one year to the next as we expend different levels of Business Energy. In other words, if you are an average go-home-and-relax-after-work person, and your BEN is low, your Income Value may be many times more than 10 percent. In that case, you have an excellent paying job despite your lack of Business Energy. But if you are one of those busybodies who is always involved in extra *business* activities for yourself and for others—increasing your BEN significantly—you may find that your Income Value is much less than what you are worth. In that case, you may want to solidify an increase of *income* that represents the continuous energy that you expend, either by increasing the prices and scope of your products and services, or by asking your present employer for a raise.

PRODUCTIVITY VALUE

To find your Productivity Value divide your Personal Income by the Company Revenue from the respective Job, Career, Goal, or History and multiply by 100 percent as documented below:

Personal Income / Company Revenue * 100% = Productivity Value

---

To calculate your Productivity Value, each individual or company must research what they or their Company grossed—or *could* gross—in Revenue for each column respectively. That is the only way to find out what your *productivity* is worth to yourself or to the company. If you own the company, your Productivity Value would be your Personal Income divided by the Revenue that your company was able to produce in your given field.

Likewise, for independent contractors and salespeople, your Productivity Value would be your Personal Income divided by the total *revenue* that you personally generated for the company from which you earned commissions. Independent contractors would include car salesman, real estate brokers, life insurance agents, or any commission positions, including any and all intellectual property based contracts such as writers, designers, architects, inventors, engineers, musicians, producers, and so on.

For a company's Productivity within a given industry, divide the Company Revenue by the Industry Revenue within a certain industry for the given year of assessment and multiply by 100 percent as documented below:

Company Revenue / Industry Revenue * 100% = Productivity Value

---

To calculate the Productivity Value of a company within a given industry, each company must research what their given industry grossed in Revenue for each column respectively.

Your Productivity Value for each respective year will tell you how productive you or your company has been within a given career or industry. The 10 Percent Rule still applies, where anything over 10 percent is gravy.

An accurate assessment of your Income Value as well as your Productivity Value will reveal that, in some cases, individuals and small companies may be more profitable under the umbrella of a larger employer or corporation, while others may be more profitable as stand-alone enterprises, partnerships, or companies that can determine their own *income*. That ultimate conclusion will be determined by you or your company after the full evaluation of your Equation Chart.

Progress

Once we all see how *The Equation* Chart works, you can insert estimated ratings for your Preferred Job, Career, or Company Goal, as well as your Dream Job, Career, or Company Goal, based on your acquired knowledge and ideas of *execution* within those particular fields.

The goal of progress would then be to utilize the Equation Chart to determine what options are available for the improvement of your personal or company *business*. Similarly, *The Equation* Chart should also allow you to assess the reasons for your Decline (if applicable).

In reality, *business* is in constant flux. So the key to create consistent success is to be able to understand all of the factors that affect your personal or company business and to make effective decisions that will improve your ratings based on the honest assessment of your equation. The honest data will provide you with plenty of viable research from which to make successful decisions concerning your *business* future.

POWER

With the full understanding of your personal and company charts, you should be able to ask yourself the following questions:

How do I strengthen my position within the company?
How do I strengthen the company within its industry?
Is my company strong and growing, or weak and declining?
Do I gain or lose *power* by working for the company?
How much *power* could I gain by investing in the company?
How much *power* could I gain by investing in myself?
Are any company investments or partnerships available to me?
Could the company gain from acquisitions or a possible sale?
Could I be involved in such company or personal moves of *power*?

As stated within the text, *power* is increased by maximizing our *income*, *productivity*, and *progress*. Investing in your own company, other lucrative companies, friends, partners, or intellectual property owners can increase your *power* significantly.

Having the *power* to invest, influence, and take over is what separates the successful from the masses. Understanding how to utilize *The Equation* Chart correctly can easily point us in the right directions.

Power is also gained through experience and knowledge. The more you educate yourself about personal and company gains and losses, the more you can act and react accordingly to improve your status and *income* in *business*.

RESPONSIBILITY

The decision to respond to the needs—and/or desires—of your supporters remains personally yours. But it is a lot more useful to be responsible from a position of *power*. Inversely, having a *responsibility* to ourselves, our family members, teammates, company, partners, investors, and the general community members who *support* us, also leads to *power*. And there is much less *income*, *productivity*, *progress*, or *power* to be gained from an economically weak community. Therefore, it becomes important for *purple business* people to maintain the economic viability of their supporters by reinvesting in the communities that have helped to create the health and wealth of their *business*.

IN CONCLUSION

More *business energy* is produced by the combination of Red Love in the first column, Gold Art in the second column, and Green Support in the fourth column. Although it is expected that many of us will have certain strengths within one component color, a high balance of all four colors is the surest way to produce the most energy toward Purple Business. Remember as well, that the color purple is a combination color produced by the *execution* of the other three components. Purple is the final frontier and the color of secured wealth. And to become Purple is to gain the ultimate level of *responsibility*.

Acquiring the color purple allows us the necessary *power* in which to utilize *passion* (Red), master the *art* (Gold), and build the *support* (Green) of any given project. As we continue to study, learn from, and increase our knowledge of, as well as from a number of other great *business* resources, we can all continue to challenge ourselves to make the necessary decisions that lead to success and *progress* in *business*.

The color of *business* (Purple) across the bridge of green awaits your arrival. And if you are still unable to apply or comprehend *The Equation* and desire a live explanation and demonstration to apply it to your personal business goals, or the goals of your company, please contact us (*www.TheEquationBook.com*) with more detailed questions about its use, or provide an invitation to your business community, and we will gladly accept your *love* of our *art* to *support* the increase of your *business*.

$$L / A * S = B^{TM}$$

is written in Black ink. The challenge to understand it, appreciate it, respect it, and utilize it... is now yours.

The Equation Chart	L (Love)	/ A (Art)	= QN Quotient Number	* S (Support)	= B (Business)	Income Value	Productivity Value
Option #1 Option #2	Red (N)	Gold (D)	Quotient Number	Green (RSN)	Purple (BEN)	$\frac{Income}{(BEN)} * 100\%$	$\frac{Income}{Company} * 100\%$
Present Job, Career, Goal	61	4	15.25	392,000	5,978,000	4.18%	16.45%
Preferred Job, Career, Goal	93	11	8.45	1,608,000	13,588,000	14.42%	18.27%
Dream Job, Career, Goal	50	40	1.25	1,950,000	2,188,000	194.24%	10%
Career Beginning	95	25	3.8	58,000	220,000	30%	36.67%
Career Peak	95	2	47.5	764,000	36,290,000	1.08%	11.70%
Career Decline	55	6	9.17	602,000	5,520,000	7%	21.44%

The Equation Chart

*100% / #1   *   ?   =   ?*

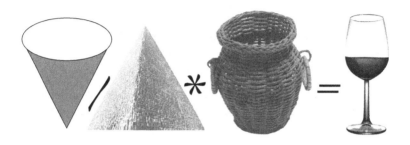

*Love / Art * Support = Business*

*L / A * S = B*

The Five Elements

Passion	Adoration	Attraction	Income
Commitment	Presentation	Packaging	Productivity
Dedication	Purpose	Organization	Progress
Loyalty	Execution	Imagery	Power
Consistency	Excellence	Movement	Responsibility

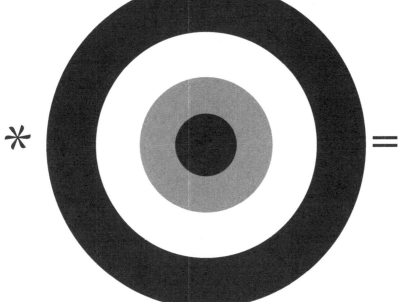

Bull's-Eye

Love   /   Art

* =

Support Business

INDEX

Printed in the United States
By Bookmasters